Singing Tree and Laughing Water

by Sylvia Hardwick

Cover and illustrations by James Converse

To Debbie

Merry Christmas 1981

Happy New Year

Love

Grandma

PACIFIC PRESS PUBLISHING ASSOCIATION
Mountain View, California

Omaha, Nebraska
Oshawa, Ontario

Chapter I

"Mrs. Grant, You'll Need Your Walking Shoes"

A long, grayish-green station wagon sped up and around the steep passes of the Cascade Range of southern Oregon. On each side of the station wagon an official-looking, gold-colored seal bore the words "State of Oregon." Three ladies sat in the front seat, and in the back seat two tawny-skinned little girls stared out the windows at the blur of giant ponderosa pine trees and Douglas firs that seemed to whiz past them. Tangled black hair hung limply to their shoulders, and their dark eyes glistened behind pools of tears that spilled over and trickled down their cheeks.

The younger of the girls, five-year-old Singing Tree, turned to her sister, who was two years older than she. "Laughing Water, will our new mamma spank us?"

Laughing Water did not say a word in reply. She did not even turn her head. She just gulped as though a big lump had stuck in her throat, and a fresh stream of tears spurted down her cheeks and dripped from her chin onto a pretty blue-and-red dress.

"Come, now, girls," the lady sitting in the middle of the front seat said, twisting sideways to see them better. "Why are you even thinking such unhappy thoughts? Mrs. Grant will be a very kind mamma, and Mr. Grant is a teacher in the junior high school; so you can be sure he likes having young people around."

"And think how nice it will be having a new big sister and two big brothers," said the lady who was driving.

"I don't want a new mother!" snapped Singing Tree. "I don't want a new sister or brothers. I want Mrs. Mahoney! She was a good mother."

And the little girl's sobs grew louder as she remembered how just a few hours before her foster mother, Mrs. Mahoney, had

3

knelt at the door of the station wagon and wept as her arms circled the two girls for a last good-bye hug. Singing Tree could still hear the cries of her four foster sisters:

"We will never see Laughing Water and Singing Tree again!"
"Where are they going?"
"What will we do without them?"
"Don't go, Singing Tree!"

The ladies in the front seat tried to think of happy things to cheer the girls; but the more they said about the new family the more Singing Tree remembered Mrs. Mahoney and her foster sisters; and the more she remembered them the harder she sobbed. Laughing Water, still staring tight-lipped and silent through the window, also seemed determined to remain unhappy.

The station wagon purred around a curve and down a long hill that led to a valley where bright green fields and the white and pink blossoms of pear and peach orchards made a dazzling patchwork in the spring sunshine. Now the driver steered off the highway onto a side road and passed under a black railroad bridge just as a long Southern Pacific train thundered by overhead. The two little girls threw themselves into each other's arms and clung together, terrified by the loud rumbling and grating. They had never before heard a train pass overhead.

The driver glanced back at the girls with a reassuring smile. "Don't let that worry you, girls. Nothing is going to hurt you. Come, now, we'll soon be there. Don't you think you could manage a happier face for your nice new mamma? She and her family have been waiting for a long time to share their home with some children who need a home, and they are particularly pleased to be able to share it with two little Indian girls like yourselves."

A spark of interest lighted Singing Tree's eyes, and she pulled away from her sister and returned to her side of the seat. "Why? Why does she want little Indian girls?"

"Mr. and Mrs. Grant came to this country from a faraway land many years ago," the lady answered. "And they decided right away they wanted to learn all they could about our beautiful country. One of the first things they started studying was the history of American Indians. And now they love Indians very much."

4

"Will they love us?" Singing Tree asked.

"Yes, of course they will."

The station wagon followed the back road along the bank of a fast-running river bordered by tall alders, maples, and cottonwood trees. A delicate fragrance from their lacy new pale-green leaves filled the car.

"Ah, what a lovely place to raise children!" said the lady sitting in the middle. "It's so far from the city and its bad smells and influences. I'm sure you'll soon love your new home," she said, turning again toward the back seat. "You'll have some little calves to play with and nice long grass to run in in the big fields. You'll have woods to play in behind the house, too. And this river runs near the house. I think you're lucky girls!"

Singing Tree had stopped sobbing and was gazing out the window at the tumbling river, but an occasional tear still trickled down the cheeks of Laughing Water.

"There are the mailboxes," said the driver. "We turn right here and go up the hill past four houses. The Grants live at the end of the drive."

The third lady, who had said very little, turned toward the girls now. "Come, dears, dry those tears. Here are some tissues." She drew Singing Tree's face close and wiped away the last traces of tears, but Laughing Water refused to be touched. She took care of the tears herself with the back of her hands.

The station wagon drew up beside a large house of knotty pine wood. It stood back from green fields where several calves played in the sunshine, and behind it rose a wooded hill.

As the little Indians climbed out of the car, they saw a huge, fluffy white dog come bounding from the back of the house with a friendly bark. At the same time a dark-haired, rosy-cheeked woman walked down a long flight of steps that led from the front porch.

"Mrs. Grant?" one of the women said, moving forward with outstretched hands. "I'm Mrs. Mason, the girls' new caseworker. You know Mrs. Molloy, the girls' former caseworker, and Mrs. Bligh came along to help us with the girls." The ladies shook hands, then Mrs. Grant turned with a smile to the little Indians.

5

"And how are you two this lovely day?" she asked holding her hands out to them. "Did you have a good trip over the mountains?"

Laughing Water stood straight and stiff, her face creased with fear and worry, and her lips pressed tightly together. Singing Tree, her chattery way getting the best of her, said, "You're our new mamma, aren't you? They told us we would be getting a nice new mamma."

"Yes, I'm your new mamma," Mrs. Grant said. "We have been waiting a long, long time for a little girl, and now we have two. And you know what? I think everything is going to be all right. Let's go inside and visit for a while."

In the fun of climbing up the long flight of stairs, Singing Tree forgot to be sad. At the top of the stairs she discovered a most delightful thing: When she pressed the doorbell button, it produced the sweetest chimes she had ever heard! Singing Tree practiced for several minutes on those chimes while Laughing Water stood at the bottom of the steps and watched. The ladies walked inside the house, pretending to ignore the girls.

When Singing Tree grew tired of the door chimes, she ran back down to the bottom of the steps, then up to the porch and back down again. She ran up and down the stairs at least twenty times. Her eyes sparkled now, and she giggled while at the same time panting for breath. "Come on, Sissy," she said to Laughing Water. "This is fun, up and down, up and down. Come on! See what fun it is," she coaxed.

Laughing Water climbed up a few steps, then her feet began to move faster and faster as she flew up and down the stairs with Singing Tree beside her. Lady, the big white dog, bounded between them, sometimes almost sending them flying to the ground.

Finally the girls ran out of breath and sat down on the bottom steps, puffing and panting, but dreading to go into the house. Then Singing Tree noticed the wide concrete sidewalk that ran along the front of the house and down the side. "Come on, Sissy," she said. "Let's see where this leads." They followed the sidewalk across the front and along the side of the house. Here and there a step or two interrupted where the ground rose higher or dropped lower. They began to run when they rounded a turn and the sidewalk

6

led along the back of the house. Up and down a few more steps, and then the sidewalk led them along the other side of the house and around one more turn until, before they realized it, they ran almost headlong into the front porch.

"Look where we are again!" Singing Tree squealed in surprise. "Back at this mountain of steps."

The girls were so tired now that they could run no more. So very slowly and quietly they climbed up the steps and slipped through the front door. The ladies sat on big soft chairs in the living room. The girls sat down on the hearth of a white fireplace that stretched along one wall of the room.

"Well, did you have a nice run?" Mrs. Mason asked, but the girls remained silent. "We were just getting ready to leave," the lady continued. "We have already helped Mrs. Grant bring all your clothes and toys in from the station wagon." Then Mrs. Mason turned to Mrs. Grant. "I know the girls will love it here once the strangeness wears off. I'm sure you will need a lot of patience, of course, but time will help. I have a feeling, Mrs. Grant, that you'll need a good pair of walking shoes to keep up with the two of them, but especially the little one. You just wait and see!"

The two little Indians watched through the front window as the station wagon disappeared in a swirl of dust. Now they were alone with their new mother. Fear showed in their eyes, and Laughing Water's chin quivered as though she would burst into tears at any moment.

"I'm sure you're very hungry," Mrs. Grant said. "We'll find your play clothes, and while you change I'll fix some soup and toast for you. How will that be?"

"Fine," responded Singing Tree; but Laughing Water could find no answer.

After sipping a few spoonfuls of soup, the girls sat quietly at the table, doing nothing.

"You may leave it if you don't feel like eating," Mrs. Grant told them. "Maybe by dinnertime when Jamey and Celia and Daddy come home from school you'll feel hungry. How would you like to help me to unpack your clothes? Afterward you could have some fun bathing your papooses."

7

"Papooses?" asked Singing Tree, while Laughing Water looked extremely puzzled.

Mrs. Grant searched the children's faces. "You mean that you are little Indians and you don't know what a papoose is?"

The children wagged their heads sideways, meaning No.

"Not very long ago you were both papooses," the new mother said, "little baby Indians; that's what papooses are. I used to know a little song about a papoose. I think I can remember most of it; I know you'd really like it."

Sitting at the piano in the living room, Mrs. Grant played and sang while the girls listened and watched:

"Wawatisi, my papoose,
Close your coal-black eyes;
Manitou is watching,
Watching from the skies;
Sleep the while the west wind
Rocks your deerskin bed;
Wawatisi, my papoose,
Rest your tiny head."

Two sets of eyes as black as Wawatisi's watched Mrs. Grant with wonder. The gentle words and sweet music made them forget their loneliness and misery for one brief moment.

"Someday soon I shall teach you that little song," Mrs. Grant promised. "Then you can sing it to the dolls when you want them to go to sleep."

When they had helped Mrs. Grant unpack all their clothes and hang them in the closet, Mrs. Grant found two large bread pans for the girls to bathe their dolls in while she made pastry for apple pies.

"Did the little papooses have dolls like we have to play with?" asked Singing Tree as she scrubbed the skin of her blond-haired baby.

"No, not like yours," said Mrs. Grant. "Their mothers and daddies carved babies for them out of wood or corncobs or stone, and the mothers made little clothes for the dolls out of deerskins

8

or rabbit fur or woven roots, just as they made clothes for the members of their families. I'm sure the little Indian girls really loved the bright-colored beads and shells and porcupine quills their mothers stitched on the baby doll clothes."

Singing Tree grew more interested. "Mamma, did the papooses have beds like ours?"

"No," Mrs. Grant answered, "the mothers strapped the babies to cradle boards which they sometimes used to carry the babies on their backs. They wrapped cozy little covers of furs and deerskins or woven roots around the papooses to keep them warm and comfortable. Don't you think it would be fun for the babies to ride around with their mothers all day?"

"Am I too big to ride around on your back all day, Mamma?" asked Singing Tree with a hopeful look.

"I'm afraid so," laughed Mrs. Grant. "Think how tired Mamma would be after carrying a big girl like you around all day!"

Mrs. Grant cut two lumps of pastry from the big ball she had mixed in the bowl. "Here," she said, "I have something really nice for you to do now. You may have these pieces of pastry dough. In a few minutes I will be finished with my rolling pin, and there is another one in the drawer; so there will be one for each of you to use to make your own little pies for supper."

A faint gleam of interest caught in Laughing Water's eyes as she took the dough from Mrs. Grant. Singing Tree began immediately to squash the dough with her hand. After Mrs. Grant had placed her apple pies in the hot oven, she gave the girls a round pie pan each in which they could place their pastry when it was ready. She showed them how to make little men with raisins for eyes, noses, and mouths and for rows of buttons on their coats.

When at last the pies were sizzling and bubbling in the oven, in walked Celia, Jamey, and Mr. Grant.

"Look at what we have here," said Mrs. Grant with a broad smile for her family.

"Two of them! Two little Indians!" Mr. Grant looked pleased.

"Our new mamma said you have been waiting for a little Indian for a long time. Are you glad there are two of us here at last?" asked Singing Tree.

9

*The first day in their new home the two little Indians helped
Mrs. Grant to bake some apple pies for supper.*

"I'll say we are," said Mr. Grant; and Celia and Jamey nodded and smiled.

"Where's the other big brother?" asked Singing Tree. "The lady in the station wagon said there was another big brother."

"He's away from home," Celia answered. "He's away at college."

"That's a school for big grown-up girls and boys," Jamey explained when he saw their puzzled looks.

When Mrs. Grant had served dinner and the family sat at the table, each one bowed his head and closed his eyes. "Dear Father in heaven," said Jamey, "thank You for this nice food. Bless it to make us well and strong, for Jesus' sake. Amen."

The new children looked from bowed head to bowed head and their mouths opened in surprise. What a strange brother Jamey was! In fact, everyone and everything in this big house seemed strange! Great waves of longing for the comfort of Mrs. Mahoney's kitchen full of noisy Indian sisters swept over the little strangers. Though they had eaten practically nothing all day, they could not eat their dinner. Not even the sweet-smelling little raisin men could tempt them.

After dinner Jamey tried to coax the girls into a happier mood. "Would you like me to show you how to make a tepee out of old blankets?" he asked.

The girls stared at Jamey with eyes that looked as round as saucers. "What's a tepee?" Singing Tree asked.

It was Jamey's turn to stare. "You mean you are two little Indians and you don't know what a tepee is?"

He went to the living room and pulled a big red book from a shelf. He looked through it until he found the page he wanted. "Here it is," he said. "Let's go out and I'll show you a picture of a tepee."

Once seated on the lawn with a little Indian on each side of him, Jamey showed them the picture. "See?" he said. "A tepee is a house, something like a tent, that the plains Indians used."

Singing Tree frowned. "What's plains Indians?" she asked.

"They were the Indians who lived a long way from here on ground that was flat in most places. That ground is called the plains or the prairies."

"Were they old-fashioned Indians?" asked Singing Tree.

11

Jamey nodded. "Sometime we'll tell you about the plains Indians," he said, "but right now we'll make the tepee."

He carefully stuck into the ground some poles, which had been used for bean poles in the vegetable garden. He joined them in a point at the top; then he covered this frame with old blankets.

"Go on inside now and play," Jamey suggested. "You can pretend you are old-fashioned Indians while I do my homework. No, wait," he added. "I almost forgot that I should feed the baby calves first. Do you want to help me?"

As the girls helped Jamey, Singing Tree said, "I wish I could be a baby calf and suck warm milk out of a big bucket. Look at the way their tails waggle; they're happy!"

That night Celia helped the girls bathe; and when they had put on their soft blue pajamas, Mrs. Grant came to their room to say good-night.

"Would you like to say prayers with me?" she asked. Dark, puzzled eyes stared at her. The little Indians did not know what the word "prayers" meant. What a strange, lonely world it had suddenly become!

"All right, then," Mrs. Grant said, "perhaps some other time we'll say prayers together." She kissed each of them on the forehead and said, "If you wake up in the night and need me, all you have to do is come along the hall to my bedroom and call me. I shall leave the night-light on in the hall so you can see your way."

"We want our music boxes," Singing Tree said. "They are in the big toy box."

The music boxes were small pink and blue merry-go-rounds made of plastic with little gray prancing horses which went around and around and up and down as the music played. Laughing Water wound hers, and the little ponies began to move in time with the music. When it sighed to a finish, Singing Tree wound her music box and set her ponies prancing to a different tune.

But before the second box stopped playing, the little Indians had begun to weep. Nothing could stop the aching and the longing within them.

"We want to go back to Mrs. Mahoney's!" cried Singing Tree.

"You try to go to sleep now," Mrs. Grant said. "I think things will seem much better in the morning."

The children continued crying for a long time; but at last, very tired, they fell asleep. Much later in the evening, when Mrs. Grant tiptoed into the bedroom to make sure the girls were covered, she stood for several minutes looking at first one and then the other of the two tiny, golden-skinned children. Tears coursed down her cheeks as she watched the warm little bodies rise and fall in restless slumber. "Dear Lord, they are Your poor little heartbroken lambs," she whispered. "Please help us to love them, and help them to love us in return; but most of all, may we teach them to love You."

Chapter 2

A Stolen Dog and a Space Trip

When the children awoke the next morning, they could hear the chirping of birds in the tree outside the window and the clinking of dishes and silverware coming from the kitchen. Rich, spicy smells sneaked under their bedroom door, but neither of them felt like eating.

"We will never see the Mahoneys and our Indian sisters again," moaned Laughing Water. "Unless—."

"Unless what?" asked Singing Tree.

"Unless we run away. We can do that if we try. If we hurry and get dressed, we can leave while everyone is still eating breakfast. I hate this big house! I don't want to stay here!"

As the girls dressed quickly in their play clothes, Mrs. Grant peeked in. "Well, you're awake at last!" she said with a cheerful smile. "You must have been very tired little Indians; you slept a long time."

"We don't want to stay here," announced Singing Tree. "We liked living with Mrs. Mahoney, and we don't like it here. Laughing Water said we can run away."

Laughing Water glared angrily at her sister for giving away the secret.

Mrs. Grant said, "I know that you are very lonely for your other home, and I'm sorry that Mrs. Mahoney was too tired and ill to look after you anymore, but this family will love you and always take good care of you. Perhaps after a while you will begin to like living here. Come, now, finish dressing and eat some breakfast."

Although the scrambled eggs and toast which Mrs. Grant had prepared for the girls looked good and smelled delicious, neither of them could get past the first mouthful. When the rest of the family

14

had gone to school, Mrs. Grant said, "All right, if you don't feel like eating, we'll put the food away and wash the dishes."

"I don't know how," said Singing Tree, while Laughing Water fixed her new mother with a gloomy stare. Mrs. Grant pretended she did not notice the stare as she showed the girls how to wash dishes. Singing Tree saw Mrs. Grant's arm close to hers as they dipped into the sudsy water.

"I wish I had a nice white arm like my new mamma's arm," she said. "Look at my ugly brown arm."

"Oh, no," said Mrs. Grant quickly. "It isn't an ugly brown arm at all. I think I would like nice brown arms, just like yours."

Both girls looked carefully at Mrs. Grant, trying to decide if she really meant what she said.

"All the other people have white arms too," persisted Singing Tree. "I want to be like the other people; I don't want to be Indian."

When the dishes were finished, Mrs. Grant drew the girls close to her. Singing Tree leaned against her new mother, wanting to feel her warmth and softness; but Laughing Water pulled away and moved across the kitchen.

"I don't want my little Indians ever to feel ashamed and unhappy about the color of their skin," she said. "It is beautiful skin. Did you know that long, long ago there were no people with white skins living in this big country of America?"

Laughing Water spun around and stared at Mrs. Grant with unbelieving eyes. Singing Tree said, "No people with white skins?"

"That's right," Mrs. Grant said. "This was Indian land; white people came a long time later to make their homes here. When they came, many of the Indians and white people were kind to each other, but others were mean and cruel and fought horrible wars. The Indians became afraid that there would be nothing for them to eat when they saw the white men clearing away the trees from the grounds where they hunted food; so they fought with the white men, hoping to scare them away. Then the white men did become afraid of the Indians who sometimes burned their homes and even killed their families. But instead of running away,

15

as the Indians had hoped, the white men turned cruel toward the Indians. At last so many white people came that they outnumbered the Indians until the Indians did not want to fight for their land anymore. Some of the Indians used to live right here where we live now. On Table Rock Mountain, just over the hills from here, the white people and the Indians promised each other that they would not fight any more wars. Sometimes people who like to go hunting for arrowheads find them along our riverbanks."

"What are arrowheads?" asked Singing Tree.

"Sometime I will tell you about the arrowheads," Mrs. Grant promised, "but right now I must get some work done. There is one thing I want you to remember, and that is that you must not feel ashamed of the color of your skin. When I tell you more about the old-fashioned Indians, I think you will see why you should feel pleased that you belong to the big Indian family. I am sure that God does not want little Indians to feel bad about the color of their skin."

"Who is God?" asked Singing Tree, wondering how many more questions she would have to ask before she understood all that her new mother told her.

"Do you remember the song Mamma sang for you yesterday? It said, 'Manitou is watching.' There is a kind Father of all people who loves us and cares for us. The old-fashioned Indians called Him Manitou. We call Him God."

"Oh," said Singing Tree. Then she paused for a moment. "Does He love Laughing Water and me?"

"He most certainly does," said Mrs. Grant. "He cares very much about both of you. He especially loves little children."

Mrs. Grant paused and looked toward the back door. "Listen!" she whispered. "I hear something!" She seemed very excited. She hurried to the back porch and stood quietly without moving. The two children followed. A gray-brown bird sat on the back fence saying, "Chap! Chap! Chap!" in a scolding tone. Mrs. Grant put a finger to her lips.

"What's the matter, Mamma?" asked Singing Tree. Neither of the girls could understand why their new mother could become so excited over a little bird on a fence.

16

"That's a little kingbird," Mrs. Grant whispered. "She has come to see us for four springs now. We leave little strips of cloth and yarn and string on the clothesline or on bushes for her to take away to build her nest."

The bird swooped to catch a moth; and as she turned, the girls saw her yellow breast. "That yellow is pretty, Mamma," said Singing Tree, "but I wouldn't like to eat moths; the taste would be horrible. Who made the kingbird?"

"The kind Father I was just telling you about," Mrs. Grant said. "He made all things that live."

"He made even me and Laughing Water and you?"

"That's right, even us," said Mrs. Grant.

She took the girls into the kitchen and showed them how to tear narrow strips from an old piece of sheet so that they would not be too long or too heavy for the kingbird to carry to the tree where she planned to build her nest. Then Mrs. Grant showed them how to hang the strips lightly in the manzanita branches so that the bird would not have to struggle to get them free. When they had hung all the strips, Mrs. Grant said, "Let us watch through the window. If we keep very still and quiet, I think the bird will come and get the cloth."

"Chap! Chap! Chap!" called the bird, looking about to make sure no enemy was near to hurt her. She flew from the fence, pecked at one of the strips; then, taking it in her beak, she flew up and away, with it trailing behind her in the breeze.

"She got it!" Laughing Water squealed, as excited as could be.

"You talked!" cried Singing Tree. "You wouldn't talk to our new mother before! Now you talked! Will you like our new mamma, now?"

A scowl spread across Laughing Water's face, and she did not answer her sister.

The kingbird and her mate came back again and again to the manzanita bush. He watched and chattered while she grabbed the strips of cloth in her beak; then both would sail away to the top of a small oak tree which could be seen from the kitchen.

When Jamey and Celia came home that afternoon, they seemed as excited as their mother when they heard that the kingbirds

17

had returned. They took the girls with them to the oak tree to watch what was going on. Dozens of streamers which Mrs. Kingbird had plucked from the manzanita branches hung from the nest and blew in the breeze that sighed through the branches of the oak tree. Now Mrs. Kingbird was scolding her mate in the meanest bird language the girls could imagine.

"What is she saying?" Singing Tree asked.

"She seems to be grumbling that, after all the planning, this does not seem to be the best place in the world to build a nest," Jamey said.

"I hope that she will make her nest look tidier than it is now," Celia said. "I'd say she is a really sloppy housekeeper!"

"Don't worry," Jamey replied. "When she gets around to it she will tuck in all the ends and have the nest looking quite neat. She always has, anyway, the other times when she built her nest here."

On the second day that the small Indians were with their new family, Mrs. Grant told Laughing Water that she would begin school that day. So Mrs. Grant and Singing Tree walked with Laughing Water to school. The lonely and frightened little girl stood very still by the teacher's desk, her drooping eyes staring at the floor and her hands clasped tightly in front of her. The teacher soon found some girls and boys to play with her, but Laughing Water would not play.

"Perhaps you should return home now," the teacher told Mrs. Grant. "I think in a few days we will be able to help Laughing Water to feel at ease."

Now Mrs. Grant and Singing Tree were the only members of the family at home. Mrs. Grant was waxing the kitchen and dining-room floors when she realized that everything in the house was quiet. "Singing Tree?" she called, but there was no answer.

Mrs. Grant thought, "I suppose I should put on my walking shoes and walk through the woods; perhaps I'll find her there, for she has been talking about how she would like to play in the woods."

As she was tying one of her shoelaces, the telephone rang and Mr. Parsons, one of the near neighbors, said, "Mrs. Grant, a little

Indian just came to my place and stole my dog. Do *you* own a little Indian?"

Mrs. Grant gasped. "Why—yes, I own a little Indian. She *stole* your *dog?* How could a little girl steal a dog, Mr. Parsons? Especially one as big as yours?"

"It seemed quite simple," Mr. Parsons said. "She just came down here, playing around, while I was making some frames for my beehives. Suddenly she disappeared. I looked about to see where she had gone, and I saw her with my dog, leading him by the chain from my property to yours; I watched her fasten the chain to a branch of the big oak tree in your middle pasture."

"Oh, dear!" gasped Mrs. Grant. "This is terrible. I'm really sorry, Mr. Parsons. How could she *think* of doing such a thing! I will certainly see that she doesn't do anything like that again. Thank you for calling me."

"Don't worry about the dog," said Mr. Parsons. "I'll bring him back and tie him in his kennel."

When Singing Tree heard Mrs. Grant calling she strolled slowly home, humming a little tune.

"Where have you been, Singing Tree?" asked Mrs. Grant.

"For a nice walk," Singing Tree answered with a smile. "I talked to the bee man. He has lots of buzzy bees that make honey for him to eat. He told me how the bees make the honey, and he says they are very clever, those bees."

"What did you do at the bee man's house?" asked Mrs. Grant.

"Nothing, betcept what I said. I like the bee man."

"You did something else," prodded Mrs. Grant. "Did you see his nice big black Labrador?"

"What's a Labrador, Mamma?" Singing Tree asked. Her head drooped, and her eyes could not meet her new mother's eyes.

"A Labrador is a kind of dog. Mr. Parsons said you took his dog and tied it to the oak tree in the middle pasture. Why did you do that?"

"Who is Mr. Parsons? I don't know Mr. Parsons."

Mrs. Grant took the little golden-brown chin in her hands and forced the black eyes to meet hers. "Why did you take Mr. Parsons' dog?"

19

"It's a nice dog!" cried Singing Tree. "I like that dog, and I want him, so I brought him home!"

"Dear! Dear!" said Mrs. Grant. "You cannot bring someone else's things home just because you like them. The dog belongs to Mr. Parsons. Would you be happy if Mr. Parsons stole your toys?"

Singing Tree said, "I like that dog. He's a nice dog, and I know he likes me because he kissed my face with his big pink tongue. Mr. Parsons is a big man and he doesn't like toys, so he wouldn't come and take my toys; but I want his dog!"

"You already have a dog," Mrs. Grant reminded the little girl. "Lady is your dog, now that you live here. She is a good dog, and if you treat her kindly she will soon learn to love you."

"Is she a Labrador?" Singing Tree asked.

"No, she is called a Husky."

Mrs. Grant took Singing Tree on her lap. "We never should take other people's things—not ever," she said. "It is very unkind to take something that belongs to someone else. It makes people feel sad and unhappy when someone steals the things which belong to them. Will you remember that?"

"Yes, Mamma, I'll try to redember. Do reindeers eat eggs?"

"Oh, no!" moaned Mrs. Grant, wondering if Singing Tree had heard a word she had said. "What made you think reindeers might eat eggs?"

"Laughing Water said they must, else how would they get such big horns?"

Thinking "Oh, I give up!" Mrs. Grant said, "Look, I have a nice job for you to do. How would you like to put the postage stamps on my letters?"

"Goody! Goody!" chanted Singing Tree, all smiles. Mrs. Grant took several minutes to show Singing Tree how to place the stamps the right way up and where they should go on the envelopes.

"The glue tastes yummy!" said Singing Tree, smacking her lips.

When the job was finished Mrs. Grant said, "Now you play until I have finished cleaning the bathroom."

When Mrs. Grant was ready to go to the post office to mail her seven letters, there were only two to be found in the letter holder on her desk. "Oh," she sighed. "Whatever could have happened to those other letters? Where can they be? I wonder—"

"Singing Tree, where are you?" she called. "Singing Tree!"

She walked to the window and saw a black head bobbing about above the tallest grass in the field. With the help of big white Lady, Singing Tree was making a roundup of all the calves. Although Mrs. Grant yelled as loud as she could, no response came from the little Indian.

Tired of the roundup at last, Singing Tree and Lady trotted home together.

"Did you hear me calling?" Mrs. Grant asked.

The dark head drooped. "No, Mamma."

"Singing Tree, did you hear me calling you when you were in the field with Lady?"

There was no answer.

"Singing Tree!"

Two large tears spilled out of the black eyes and crept down the chubby brown cheeks.

"I was having the bestest fun. I was an Indian cowgirl," explained Singing Tree between choking noises. "Lady was my white horse; it was lots of fun."

"Did Mrs. Mahoney tell you to come when you are called—every time you are called?"

"No," said Singing Tree, brightening. "She did not care if we didn't come. She gave us lots of chances."

Mrs. Grant looked very severe. "I will not give you lots of chances," she said. "You must come as soon as I call you. Do you understand? I want both of my little Indians to be very obedient."

"What's obedient?" asked Singing Tree.

"It is doing everything you are told to do when you are told, and coming when you are called. Did you touch Mamma's letters?"

The big eyes lowered as the black head drooped again.

"Where are my letters?" asked Mrs. Grant.

"I mailed them."

"You mailed them? Where?"

"In the washing machine."

"Oh, you couldn't have!" moaned Mrs. Grant, thinking of the

21

hours she had spent writing the letters as she raced down the basement stairs, towing Singing Tree by her dirty little fist. Singing Tree opened the door of the big automatic washing machine and pulled out the letters. Fortunately for Mrs. Grant they were dry.

"You may mail them at the post office in the right way," she said. "But never, never take Mamma's letters and mail them anywhere else. The mail carrier would never find them in the washing machine. Mamma's letters are all very important, and I certainly don't want to have them lost and have to write them all again."

"What's inportent?" asked Singing Tree.

"The word is *important*," said Mrs. Grant. "When we say something is important we mean that it is very *special*. Something that is not for little girls to play with. Do you understand?"

In the afternoon Mrs. Grant wanted to take a short nap. To Singing Tree she said, "Now, you stay on your bed and rest. When it is time for you to get up, I will call you. Do you understand? Stay there on your bed until I call you."

"Yes, Mamma."

Mrs. Grant did not find Singing Tree on her bed when she rose from her nap. Going through every room, she called and called but heard no answer. She looked out in the field; the calves grazed contentedly, but no Singing Tree was to be seen.

"Oh, dear!" she said worriedly, racing to the closet where she kept her sturdy brown walking shoes. "I guess the caseworker was right; one thing I really need where Singing Tree is concerned is a good pair of walking shoes."

She ran to Mr. Parsons' house and to his honey shed, but it was empty. Mr. Parsons was not at home. She ran through the trails in the back woods calling and calling, but all she heard in reply was the soft sighing of the spring breeze in the trees and two blue jays having a loud quarrel.

Mrs. Grant stopped a moment and breathed a quick prayer. "Dear Father in heaven, please help me to find the little Indian— Oh, I just can't imagine where she would be this time!"

When she reached the house again, she was all out of breath and her legs felt weak. Flopping into a kitchen chair to recover a little before continuing the search, she heard, Thump! Thump! Thump!

"That must be Singing Tree hitting the front of the house with a big stick," she thought and raced to the front of the house, but she found no Singing Tree and no big stick. She ran to the side of the house; still no Singing Tree. But there was the Thump! Thump! Thump! again. She raced into the basement. Thump! Thump! Thump! Oh, where could that be coming from? She opened the washing-machine door. The machine was empty. She opened the front of the clothes dryer. Singing Tree was crouched in the drum of the dryer looking tired and frightened. Her red eyes told Mrs. Grant that she had been weeping for a long time. Mrs. Grant pulled her out; then she sat on a chair with Singing Tree on her lap. Singing Tree cried and cried and clung to her new mother.

When at last the little girl stopped crying, Mrs. Grant asked, "Why did you lock yourself in the clothes dryer?"

"I wanted to go in the space ship," Singing Tree answered. "It was like the one we saw on television at Mrs. Mahoney's house. Just the same, you know. They had fun in that space ship, so I wanted to have fun in this space ship. See?"

"Do you know that you did a dangerous thing, locking yourself in there?"

"Why was it dangress?" asked Singing Tree.

"Dangerous is the word," said Mrs. Grant. "It was dangerous because there is no food or water in there, and you cannot move around or take care of yourself. Finally your body would stop working and you would die."

"I don't want to die," said Singing Tree, her bottom lip quivering. "Why won't my body work if I don't have food and water?"

"That's just the way God made us," Mrs. Grant told her. "He made our bodies like machines, and they work only when food and water comes into them. When I could not find you, I talked to God and asked Him to help me find you, and He did. If I had not found you, you might have died."

"Did God know that I was in the dryer?"

"Yes, He did; He knows where everyone is."

23

"Mamma, is the washing machine a *he* or a *she?*" asked Singing Tree.

"Oh, NO!" breathed Mrs. Grant. "What next?"

To Singing Tree she said, "The washing machine is not a *he* or a *she*. It is not alive, so it is not one or the other."

"Oh," Singing Tree said in a tone which indicated that life seemed complicated to her.

Laughing Water came in from school looking sad and tired and cross. Mrs. Grant wanted to hug her and comfort her, but Laughing Water did not want to be touched. Only her old familiar home at Mrs. Mahoney's away across the mountains seemed comforting to her.

The rest of the family came home, each member wanting to know what kind of day Mrs. Grant had had. "Oh, dear! Don't ask me!" she sighed. "It has been *quite* a day!"

At bedtime neither of the girls could find her pajamas. Mrs. Grant and Celia helped them in a full-scale search, but they found no pajamas.

"It is too bad that we have used up all the time I planned to teach you the little papoose song," Mrs. Grant told the children. "Now it is bedtime and too late for singing."

Tears popped into four big black eyes at once.

"Tomorrow you must fold your pajamas and place them under your pillows as I showed you to do," Mrs. Grant warned. "That way, we won't lose valuable time looking for them."

Her eyes caught sight of the toy box in the corner of the bedroom. She dug through the many toys to the bottom, and came back out with two pairs of blue pajamas.

"I wonder how they could possibly get to the bottom of that big box," mused Mrs. Grant.

"That could be easy for 'jamas," Singing Tree explained. " 'Jamas has legs and legs can walk, you know, Mamma. That's what legs is for."

The girls set their music boxes in motion. The music played, the horses pranced, and two sad little Indians cried themselves to sleep.

24

Chapter 3

Pictures and Toothpaste

Singing Tree was awake, chirping with the birds at early dawn, much to the displeasure of everyone else in the house. As soon as she heard Mrs. Grant stirring in her bedroom she called out, "Mamma, Laughing Water has a real problem; she doesn't know which dress to wear to school today."

Mrs. Grant came into the room. "Considering the number of dresses she has packed in that closet, I feel sure it is a giant problem." So many dresses were crowded into that end of the closet that Mrs. Grant, when she tried, could scarcely separate them to get one out for Laughing Water.

"You girls certainly have many more clothes than the little old-fashioned Indians had long, long ago," she said. "I think those little Indian girls probably thought they were rich if they had one deerskin dress or, maybe, a blanket made of strips of rabbit fur to wrap around them in winter."

When the rest of the family left for school, Mrs. Grant decided that she could not go through another day like the last one, so she kept Singing Tree under her eyes every minute. They made beds together, dusted, washed clothes, and washed and dried dishes. Then Mrs. Grant got out her sewing. Between stitches on her own dress she showed Singing Tree how to thread a needle and how to make a knot in the end of her thread. She folded some pretty green material and showed the little girl how to make a purse for herself. Soon Singing Tree was making tiny running stitches; she was so proud and excited that she kept sliding off her chair, running to Mrs. Grant, and saying, "Look, Mamma, I can sew, can't I? Won't Laughing Water be apprised? Will you teach me to make my own dresses when I get big like Celia? Will you teach Laughing Water to sew when she comes home?"

After saying "Yes, I will" about two dozen times Mrs. Grant grew weary. She yawned and scratched her head and wondered if she would ever get her dress finished. She decided that she and Singing Tree both needed a nap.

"Now," she said in a firm tone as she put Singing Tree down on her bed, "I am very sleepy, for I was up early this morning; I want you to be extra quiet this afternoon while I rest. I think you could use a nap, but if you do not feel sleepy you may look at your picture books. You must stay on your bed until I come for you. You must not go out of your room until I come for you. Is that clear? Do you understand Mamma?"

"Yes, Mamma, I'll be good for you," Singing Tree promised. "You're a pretty, sweet Mamma like honey and I will always be good for you."

When Mrs. Grant awoke an hour later and appeared in the doorway of Singing Tree's room she rubbed her eyes just to make sure she was not still napping and dreaming. Dozens of toys were scattered all over the beds and floor, and Singing Tree sat in the middle of the mess.

"Why did you throw your toys everywhere?" Mrs. Grant asked.

"I wanted my big box of crayons," said Singing Tree. "I wanted to draw pictures." At that moment Mrs. Grant's gaze came upon the pictures Singing Tree had drawn on the newly painted cream-colored walls.

"Oh, no!" cried Mrs. Grant. "Singing Tree, you naughty, naughty girl! How could you do such a terrible thing! What will Daddy say?"

"It wasn't a terrible thing I did, Mamma," Singing Tree said brightly. "It was fun, and it was nice. We didn't had a nice clean wall at Mrs. Mahoney's place to draw pictures on. This is a very nice place for little kids to have fun drawing pictures."

Mrs. Grant looked as though she might weep at any minute. She went to the kitchen and came back with an eraser and a wet cloth. Trying the eraser on a piece of drawing, she felt pleased with the way it removed the crayon.

26

"All right," she said, "you take this eraser and begin rubbing hard. We must get the walls clean before Daddy gets home. He worked very hard to build our house. He painted your room so it would be pretty. He would be very unhappy if he could see it now."

Both worked hard. Soon the little Indian's arms grew tired as she rubbed and rubbed at the walls. She began to weep.

"I can't do it, Mamma," she sobbed. "It's too hard. I wish I didn't draw on the walls."

"That's what I wish too," said Mrs. Grant. "I have many other things to do, and helping you is really wasting my time. If you do this again, I won't help you rub off the marks; you will have to do it all by yourself. Do you understand?"

For answer, Singing Tree cried harder and louder.

Later when Mrs. Grant was working in the kitchen, she became aware of a sudden silence. Then Singing Tree called, "Mamma, will you make us some instinct pudding? I like instinct pudding very much. It is my most favoritist thing to eat."

"It happens to be instant pudding, not instinct pudding," Mrs. Grant said. "Instant means that you can make it right away without having to cook it. Instinct refers to things like when the bees go out to gather honey from the flowers and then can find their way back to their nests. Something tells them how to go back, and this knowledge is called instinct."

"I thought you told us God tells things what to do," called Singing Tree from her room.

"Yes, I did," said Mrs. Grant. "God tells them through their instincts."

Mrs. Grant examined the walls and found them to be almost as good as new. She touched them up here and there where a few marks were still showing.

"How are you today?" Mrs. Grant asked Laughing Water when she came in from school. Laughing Water frowned and pulled away from her new mother.

"Change your clothes and we'll put out some more strips of cloth," Mrs. Grant said. "The little bird has taken away the last of the others we put out and has been sitting on the fence, scolding because we haven't given her some more."

As soon as Mrs. Kingbird saw the new streamers fluttering on the manzanita by the kitchen fence, she grew excited and made loud noises. She hurried away, bringing back Father Kingbird to show him the wonderful thing that had happened.

Mrs. Grant and the girls watched from the kitchen window. "I think," Mrs. Grant said, "that what she is saying is, 'We need to hurry to get our nest ready so that I can lay my eggs.'"

The girls liked that idea, and they both laughed. For the first time since the children came, Mrs. Grant saw what a good name had been chosen for Laughing Water. Her laughter rippled and bubbled in clear, sweet tones like fast waters running over rocks and pebbles. To Mrs. Grant it was about the loveliest sound in the world!

"I have time to take you for a walk in the woods before I start to get dinner ready," Mrs. Grant said as she went to the closet to get out her walking shoes.

As they began their walk she said, "One thing I want you to remember is that you must not go walking in the woods alone; you might become lost. Wild animals prowl around farther back in these woods. I don't ever want you to go anywhere unless one of our family is with you. Do you understand?"

They soon came to a cleared place in the woods where a big pile of wood shavings had once lain. Now just a scattering of them remained.

"Look!" cried Singing Tree. "Little houses!"

Mrs. Grant told the girls that Richard, Celia, and Jamey had played here when they were little children. "They made little villages from blocks of wood and bricks. They made logging-truck roads and lumber mills. Richard owned a large toy logging truck which he pulled along the tiny roads, carrying logs to the lumber mills."

"We want to make a village like they made," said Singing Tree. "Will you show us how to do it?"

"I'd like to make a village like the old-fashioned Indians used to make," Laughing Water said.

28

"Sister talked," cried Singing Tree. "She must be getting happy."

Mrs. Grant looked about, finding bricks and pieces of pumice blocks which her children had played with years before.

"These would be just the right thing to show you how to make an Indian pueblo," she smiled. "They were the villages made by the desert Indians, you know. How would you like that?"

Both little Indians clapped their hands and did a little dance. "No one ever showed us how to make an old-fashioned Indian village," Singing Tree said.

"The Pueblo Indians lived far away from here in the desert," Mrs. Grant said. "The desert is a hot place; very sandy and very dry and dusty. Practically no trees grow there."

She began stacking pumice blocks, one on the other until she saw that they reached the height she wanted.

"Why do you put them like that?" Singing Tree asked. "Did they have *high* houses?"

"Yes," answered Mrs. Grant. "They made high houses from mud bricks, without doors, so that their enemies could not come into their homes easily. They left holes in the roofs and let down ladders so that their own people could go in and out as they pleased."

"They had a good idea," Laughing Water said. "They must have been clever Indians."

"What was the name of the Indians that made high houses?" Singing Tree wanted to know.

"They were the Zuñi Indians," Mrs. Grant said. "Other Indians came later and saw the nice houses and the nice gardens they made and they tried to steal their things."

"They were mean Indians to steal like that," commented Laughing Water.

"Like I stole the bee man's dog?" asked Singing Tree.

"Just like that," mused Mrs. Grant. "I hope that my Indians will never take anything that does not belong to them. If we want nice things for ourselves, we must earn them by working for them, just as Zuñi Indians did. It is a very wonderful feeling to have something for which we have worked."

After dinner Mrs. Grant and Celia took out their sewing and taught Laughing Water to do the things that Singing Tree had learned during the day. Mrs. Grant also taught them the little lullaby about Wawatisi.

Singing Tree and Laughing Water were supposed to be getting ready to go to church. Mrs. Grant peeked into the bathroom to see if they were getting their faces clean.

"Oh, no. It is not to eat!" she cried. "How much have you eaten?"

"Not much! Just this much," said Singing Tree.

"Oh, no!" moaned Mrs. Grant again, rubbing her hand over her forehead. "Toothpaste is not meant to be eaten. It is meant to clean your teeth."

"It's goody! Real goody!" chirped Singing Tree as happily as a meadowlark in spring. "It's betteren candy. Isn't it, Sister?"

Laughing Water did not answer. With her mouth full of toothpaste she quietly searched her new mother's face. Mrs. Grant took the toothpaste from Singing Tree.

"I'm taking this to my bathroom," she said in a tired voice. "When you need some I'll squeeze it for you."

In the kindergarten room at church Singing Tree wriggled and twisted and squirmed. She had never needed to sit still and quiet for so long. The pretty pictures and the stories interested her, but it seemed that nothing could be interesting enough to make her sit still for so long.

And what was happening now? she wonderd when one tiny girl said, "I'll say prayers now, teacher." All the children closed their eyes and bowed their heads. The tiny girl with the long blond curls was saying to the kind Father in heaven, "Thank You for all the good things we have. Thank You for my new baby brother and for taking care of us in the night."

"Maybe someday I will say prayers too," thought Singing Tree, "just like Mamma wanted me to."

Laughing Water sat and looked at all the strange things that were going on about her. This was not like the school she had attended the other days. She looked as perplexed as Singing Tree.

"It's goody! Real goody!" Singing Tree chirped as she and Laughing Water ate the toothpaste.

Chapter 4

Helping God With Elmer's Glue

For several days the mother kingbird took the strips of sheet from the manzanita near the kitchen window. As she worked at putting together her nest, she scolded her poor husband unmercifully until, impatient, he talked back with a loud "Chap. Chap. Chap." One bright spring day the Grants realized that things had become extremely quiet outdoors.

"Mrs. Kingbird probably has some eggs to sit on now," Jamey said to the girls. "If she doesn't sit on them to keep them warm, the babies will not hatch; they will just die in the eggs and all the birds' work will have been for nothing."

The girls soon noticed that Mrs. Kingbird had a good, attentive husband. He took care of her by catching every moth and grub his keen eyes could find and taking most of them back to the nest for his wife to eat.

Celia told the girls that the babies would come out of the eggs soon; then after they had grown strong enough, the mother would teach them to fly. "Then you'll see some real fun," Celia promised.

One day after the rest of the family had gone to school, Singing Tree helped Mrs. Grant do the morning chores. When Mrs. Grant took out the iron and ironing board to start work on a big pile of ironing, she said to Singing Tree, "You have done enough to help me now. You may go out and play on the back lawn with Lady; but don't go away, will you? Stay right there on the lawn until I call you."

"All right, Mamma, I'll be a expecially good girl for you. I'll do everything you tell me. You're a nice Mamma. I'll always be a very good girl for you."

Mrs. Grant had not finished ironing the first shirt when she heard an earsplitting scream. She raced outdoors, but Singing Tree was not on the lawn where she was supposed to be.

"Singing Tree, where are you?" cried Mrs. Grant, racing around the house. Singing Tree was nowhere to be seen, and she made no answer. Mrs. Grant's mind raced over all the places a little girl could get into trouble enough to produce such a loud scream, but she could think of nothing at first. Ah! the cows' water tank! She ran through the gate close to her bedroom window to where the tank stood beside the pasture fence.

A pair of brown legs hung over the side of the tank, kicking wildly in the air. Pudgy hands stretched out and gripped the edge of the tank, but the rest of Singing Tree hung unsteadily over the cows' cold water, her long black hair floating on top, and she was gasping for breath. Mrs. Grant rushed to the tank, pulled Singing Tree out of it, and stood her on the ground. Singing Tree, at the moment, was hardly in the mood for singing. She bellowed, and her body shook with giant sobs.

Mrs. Grant could see that Singing Tree had climbed up on the side of the tank and had sat on the rim, holding on with both hands, her back to the water and her legs swinging merrily. But she had overbalanced, and the top of her body had swung down backwards into the tank. Mrs. Grant carried the sobbing Singing Tree into the house, bathed her, and washed her hair in warm, soapy water.

"I was scared," Singing Tree said when she stopped crying. "If you didn't come I would get drowned, and then you'd have just one little Indian and not two."

"You did a very foolish and naughty thing," Mrs. Grant said as she rubbed Singing Tree's hair with the towel. "You made a big promise to Mamma that you would stay on the back lawn to play with Lady, and you didn't keep your promise. It is wrong to make promises to Mamma and then not keep them."

Birds in the large oak tree outside the girls' bedroom window made strange, twittery noises as Singing Tree and Laughing Water were getting ready for bed that night.

33

"The birds are chattery like me," said Singing Tree. "What are they saying, Mamma?"

"I think they are probably saying good night to each other," smiled Mrs. Grant.

"Why do they say good night?"

"Because they love each other, I suppose," Mrs. Grant answered. "They have had a happy day, and they are telling each other about all the wonderful things that have happened during the day. They are telling each other to be sure to have a good night's sleep, I think."

"Do they say prayers?" asked Singing Tree.

"I'm sure they must," said Mrs. Grant. "When I listen to them, I think I hear them saying, 'Thank You, God, our kind Father, for taking care of us and helping us to find enough good things to eat so that we won't be hungry.' "

"God takes care of us and gives us good things to eat, too, doesn't He, Mamma?"

"That's right," Mrs. Grant replied. "That is why people who love God like to kneel down every night and say Thank You to the kind Father."

After Mrs. Grant had tucked the small Indians into their soft beds, she taught them a song they had never heard.

" 'Jesus loves me, this I know,
For the Bible tells me so;
Little ones to Him belong;
They are weak, but He is strong."

"It is nice that He loves us," Singing Tree said sleepily as she wound up her music box to set the small horses prancing. "Mamma, how did you get to know about Jesus and we didn't?"

"I suppose no one at Mrs. Mahoney's house told you about Jesus," said Mrs. Grant. "I am sorry no one did, but I will tell you about Him. When I was a tiny, tiny girl my mother taught me about Jesus. She had found out about Him in a big black book we had, called the Bible. He was the Baby of the kind Father in heaven, and He came to this earth to teach people about His Father and how He wanted them to be kind to each other and to love one another."

"Did Jesus get borned in the hospital where Jamey and Celia and Richard got borned?" asked Singing Tree.

"Oh, no," Mrs. Grant smiled. "Jesus was born in a cow shed, and His lovely mother, Mary, made a soft little bed for Him in the hay. She loved her little Baby and took care of Him well, because she knew that the Father in heaven had special work for Him to do in showing everyone in the world how to love one another."

"If Mary loved her little Baby, why did she let Him get born in the hay?" asked Laughing Water, looking very troubled.

"Mary and her husband, Joseph, were away from their home when it was time for Jesus to be born," Mrs. Grant explained. "A lot of other people were away from their homes, too, and many of them had reached the little town where Jesus was born before Joseph and Mary got there. They had taken up all the rooms to sleep in. One kind man told Joseph he could take Mary into his shed to rest in the sweet hay, and that was where Jesus was born. I think Mary and Joseph were so tired they probably loved their bed in the cow shed."

"Did Jesus have a caseworker?" Singing Tree asked with a frown.

Mrs. Grant smiled widely. "Oh, no, He did not need a caseworker. His mother was a kind mother, always taking good care of her beautiful Baby. It is only little children who do not have mothers or whose mothers don't take good care of them who have caseworkers."

Then Mrs. Grant told the children about how it was when Jesus grew up. "He told people stories about His Father in heaven; He made sick people well, and He made blind people see again. He was very, very kind to everyone, showing all the people who saw Him how they must be to others."

"Jesus was a nice Man," said Laughing Water. "I like to hear about Him."

The next morning there were strawberries for breakfast.

Laughing Water popped a big, dark red strawberry into her mouth. A frown came over Singing Tree's face. "Daddy, do strawberries *die* when they're ate?"

SINGING TREE AND LAUGHING WATER

Mr. Grant thought a moment. "No, I suppose they don't really die. They go into little girls' bodies and help to keep the blood clean and healthy; so I suppose you could say that they go on living, being part of little girls that are alive."

"Oh," said Singing Tree as though she really understood. "Look, Lady just chased Mr. Parsons' spotted cat. It ran up the tree. Lady is standing up on her back legs, but she can't run up the tree. How can cats run up trees and dogs can't?"

Jamey said, "The cats have sharp claws that can cling to the bark of trees. They can get a hold on the tree trunks as they move. Dogs don't have the same kind of claws. The truth is that God made some animals that can climb and some animals that can't climb."

"God made cats and dogs too?"

"That's right; He made all living things."

Laughing Water said, "It looks to me as though God is pretty clever!"

"The things that God does is trenenduous," said Singing Tree, a wise glint in her eye. Everyone smiled, and Celia said, "I think you mean tremendous, don't you? Where did you hear that word?"

"Oh, I just heard Mamma say it when she was talking on the telephone yesterday," she said.

A bee zoomed through the open kitchen door.

"It is probably thinking about strawberries for breakfast," said Celia.

"How did it know that we had strawberries for breakfast?" asked Laughing Water, a puzzled frown puckering her eyebrows.

"I guess it has an extra good smeller," Mr. Grant said.

"God gave them that extra good smeller and taught them to search for their food in flowers, even ones that are far, far away from their nests," Mrs. Grant added.

"Seems to me," said Laughing Water, "that God fixes everything for all the animals and people."

Mrs. Grant was learning more and more every day that with two high-spirited little Indians in the house, life could be interesting. If she did not keep Singing Tree right under her nose while the others were away for the day, anything, just anything, was likely to happen at any moment.

One morning when she went to turn on the water for the cows' tank she found Singing Tree very busy doing something with her rosebushes under her bedroom window.

"Oh, no!" she cried when she saw that Singing Tree had in her hand a white plastic glue container. "Oh, no! You couldn't!"

But Singing Tree *could*! Apparently there wasn't very much that Singing Tree *couldn't* do!

"Why did you do it?" asked Mrs. Grant, in a trembling voice.

"I was painting the rose bushes," said Singing Tree. "Didn't you listen to the man at church? He said God paints the lovely roses and pansies. You redember?"

Mrs. Grant nodded. "Remember is the word."

"Well, we don't have pansies, but we have rosebushes, and while we are waiting for the roses to come out on the bushes I am painting the leaves. That way I am helping God. I think, now that I have painted all the leaves, the roses will come. God will be pleased I am helping Him. The lady at church said we must be God's helpers."

Mrs. Grant made a soft, groaning sound. "Oh, no!" she said. "Help God, yes, but not with Elmer's glue!"

"If I don't help Him with glue, then how do I help Him?" asked Singing Tree, surprised that her mother was not pleased with what she had done.

"In many ways," said Mrs. Grant. "By being kind to everyone, as Jesus taught us to be; by obeying mothers and fathers; by helping with the housework; and, yes, you may help God in the garden too. That is what you are doing when you help Mamma weed and water and dig, but not by painting the rosebushes with Elmer's glue!"

She tried to wipe some of the glue off the rose leaves, but already it had dried hard in the bright sunshine.

Singing Tree and Lady were covered with mud from their heads to their toes. Mrs. Grant guessed immediately what they had done.

Chapter 5

A Very Muddy Indian

"Could I meet Laughing Water at the bus today when it comes from school?" begged Singing Tree.

"I'm not sure," said Mrs. Grant. "It is a long way down the hill to the bus stop, and after all the things I have seen you do I am not sure that I can trust you out of my sight!"

"What's that mean, Mamma?" asked Singing Tree, a puzzled expression passing across her face.

"It means that you have done so many dangerous things since you came to live with us that I am afraid to let you go anywhere by yourself for fear you will get terribly hurt."

"Oh, I'll be good, Mamma," she promised, smiling one of her most charming smiles. "I'll be cepsationally good. You try me and see. You'd be very apprised."

"Play in the shade while I finish writing these letters. Get out your dollies and play house with them, and when I have finished maybe I'll have time to walk down to the bus with you."

As Mrs. Grant sealed one of her envelopes, she realized that it had been some time since she had heard Singing Tree talking to Lady and the dolls. A cold tingle shivered along Mrs. Grant's spine, though the day was sunny and warm. She ran to the door, and as she had suspected the yard was empty. She called until she thought her voice would vanish. There just wasn't any sign of an Indian or a white dog.

Thinking of all the places Singing Tree might go, she suddenly remembered Singing Tree's request to go to meet the school bus.

Jerking on the walking shoes, she raced down the hill. If Singing Tree had gone to meet the bus, she would have to pass over a wooden bridge that spanned the irrigation ditch; the bus was not due for hours. What would Singing Tree do while she waited for the bus to rattle around the bend in the road?

Mrs. Grant raced on, already picturing a little drowned Indian being dragged from the ditch. Her heart thumped like a stampede of elephants as she ran on toward the ditch.

What a sight met her eyes! "Oh, no!" she cried for about the thousandth time since Singing Tree's arrival.

"Singing Tree, you naughty, naughty girl! You promised that I could trust you—that you would be very, very good!"

The little girl's hair and clothes were soaked and dripping. Mud was plastered all over her face and arms; blobs of it clung to her clothes and were matted in her hair. Lady, her white coat full of mud, came trotting along behind. It was easy for Mrs. Grant to see what had happened, and Singing Tree's story proved her suspicions to be correct.

Lady, the kind of dog who loves plopping around in water, had gone with Singing Tree to meet the bus. The dog had taken one look at the clear, sparkling water and jumped in. It looked so easy and like such a wonderful thing to do that Singing Tree followed Lady. When she found the water coming up around her neck she grew very frightened. She began to scream, but no one could hear her. What she did not realize was that the water was not deep enough to cover her head.

She tried to climb out on the ditch bank, but the slippery mud and wet grass made her slide back into the water. She grabbed and clawed and cried until at last she struggled out on the bank. That was how she had become muddy all over.

"You could have drowned," Mrs. Grant said in a shaky voice.

"I was frightened," said Singing Tree. "I'm still scared. Give me a hug, Mamma, and then I won't be so scared."

Mrs. Grant looked at the pretty pink, clean dress she had put on before sitting down to write her letters. She looked at the muddy little Indian. "Oh, no!" she groaned to herself, but she *did*; the pink dress did not look so pink after she had held Singing Tree close to her, but Singing Tree soon felt better, and that seemed more important than the pink dress. She carried Singing Tree a short distance up the hill.

"Did your mamma carry you when you were a little girl?" asked Singing Tree.

"Yes, she did," puffed Mrs. Grant, putting her down.

"You growed up big and you're your own mamma now," said the little Indian; "so now you don't need to get carried anymore."

Mrs. Grant scrubbed Singing Tree all over in a warm bath; she shampooed her hair and rinsed it until it squeaked clean. She dressed her in clean clothes and began to comb her hair.

"Good Indians don't cry when they are getting snarls combed out of their hair, do they, Mamma?" asked Singing Tree, her lip quivering because of the painful operation.

"Are you a good Indian?" asked Mrs. Grant.

"Oh, yes, Mamma, you know I'm a very good Indian," she assured. "Good Indians always get out of ditches without getting drowned."

When the time came for the bus to arrive, Mrs. Grant, in a clean dress, and Singing Tree looking as though she had never left the house all day, set off with Lady to meet the big yellow bus. Mr. Sam had been stopping every day at the same spot for many years; in fact, since before Singing Tree was born, but that did not occur to Singing Tree. She held up her little brown fist in a *halt!* gesture and cried out, "Mamma, he's not going to stop for me. You make him stop!"

The bus came to a grinding halt, and Singing Tree laughed, "Oh, I know how to make Mr. Sam stop his big bus, don't I, Mamma?"

The folding door of the bus clattered open, and before Laughing Water and the other children had time to get out Mr. Sam said, "What about it, little Indian? You want to ride to the end of the bus run with the other kids?"

Singing Tree's joy bubbled over everywhere as she jumped around, clapping her hands. "Is it all right, Mamma?" she asked.

Mrs. Grant smiled and nodded. Up the steps Singing Tree scrambled, and behind her the big folding door went s-w-i-s-h, clank!

Mrs. Grant was still waiting when the children piled off the

41

bus, all shouts and laughter, a short time later.

"It was fun on the bus, Mamma," said Singing Tree. "I'm going to make the mostest noise of all on the bus when I go to school; you see!"

In the evening the girls worked with Mr. and Mrs. Grant in the vegetable garden while Jamey and Celia did homework. The girls had never planted seeds, so they thought it was a wonderful experience to pop grains of corn and bean seeds into the little holes Mrs. Grant had made and then to cover the seeds with soft brown soil.

Mr. Grant turned on the water sprinklers after they had planted the last seed, explaining that seeds need water to help them sprout and grow. Singing Tree became very worried when she saw the soil getting wet.

"Daddy, will the sprinklers drown the garden?" she asked. "I don't want the little baby seeds to get drowned!"

Mr. Grant assured her that the seeds would not be drowned and that they needed the water to drink.

As Mr. Grant gathered the tools, Mrs. Grant said, "We have been planting seeds like the Zuñi Indians did. They worked together to make their gardens grow, and then, when the things ripened, they shared their food. I think that was the nicest way any people could live."

Just then a big black bird flew across the blue sky. "That's a crow," said Mrs. Grant. "What a noisy fellow he is! Funny that he should come over just as I was talking about the Zuñi Indians, for the little Indian boys used to have quite a job trying to keep the crows from stealing the corn that was planted. I suppose they got quite tired of chasing crows all day."

"Poor boys!" said Laughing Water. "Didn't they ever have any fun? Didn't they ever play games?"

"Of course," said Mrs. Grant. "All children everywhere have played games. The old-fashioned Indians played many games that children play these days, like hide-and-seek and follow-the-leader and tag."

"I think it must have been fun to be an old-fashioned Indian," cut in Laughing Water. "I wish I had been an old-fashioned Indian. It was much more fun than it is now."

"Not really," said Mrs. Grant. "No matter where we are or at what time we live, we can have fun or we can be miserable. It all depends on us. If we want to be happy, we will find ways to be happy; if we want to be sad, there will be plenty of reasons."

Laughing Water looked deeply into Mrs. Grant's hazel-brown eyes. She smiled then, for she understood just what those words could mean to her in her new home.

"Did those old-fashioned Indian children have pets too?" Singing Tree persisted.

"Oh, yes. Most of the pets the Indian children had were wild animals which they caught and tamed."

"If I could be a little old-fashioned Indian, I would catch a big buzzy buzzard and let him be my pet," said Singing Tree. "He would buzzy everything, and then nothing could hurt this little Indian."

When Mr. Grant went indoors, he found a stick of chewing gum for each of the girls because they had helped so well in the garden. They both laughed with delight as they took the wrappers off the gum.

"One thing I know the old-fashioned Indians' children did not have," said Laughing Water. "That was chewing gum."

"I'm afraid you are wrong," Mrs. Grant said. "They did have chewing gum made from dried milkweed sap or cattail sap or even the pitch from pine trees. Of course it did not taste like yours, and it wasn't wrapped nicely like yours, but I'm sure they enjoyed it just as much."

"Mamma, Mrs. Mason said that you and Daddy studied a lot about Indians. Is that how you know so much about little old-fashioned Indian kids?" asked Laughing Water.

"Yes, she was right," Mrs. Grant answered. "When we came to this country, we wanted to learn as much as we could about the country and its people. I still like to read about the Indians, especially now that I have two little Indians of my own."

The children disappeared while Mrs. Grant was washing the supper dishes and Mr. Grant was reading the evening newspaper.

There was no answer when Mrs. Grant called. She pulled out the good old walking shoes again. "I've certainly had plenty of exercise lately," she said to her husband. "In fact, I'd say that I've been having a little too much exercise. I'm afraid if things don't simmer down a bit my poor shoes will be worn out."

She hurried around to all the neighbors' houses. Not one person had caught a glimpse of the girls. She ran to the irrigation ditch. She walked through the woods, calling, calling. No Indians! Then she remembered that Lady was also missing; so she called her, but no Lady came.

Mrs. Grant went back to the house feeling very worried. Where, just where, could those Indians be?

Mr. Grant tried to comfort her. "When they see it is growing dark they'll come home," he said. "You know the old saying, 'Night brings the crows home'? I wouldn't worry if I were you."

"But they may be lost!" moaned Mrs. Grant. "They may have gone adventuring a little too far. I have told them a number of times not to go back into the woods alone. I have explained to them that there could be bears and mountain lions to hurt them— Oh, no!"

She stopped and stared at her husband, alarm all over her face. "You know, I just thought of those old gold mines up the hill. Do you suppose they found one of those and have gone in through the tunnel and lost their way?"

Now Mr. Grant looked anxious. "After all that Singing Tree has accomplished in the short time she has been with us, I guess they could do almost anything," he agreed, scratching his head and looking off toward the mines.

He went out to the car and tooted the horn, and Mrs. Grant called until she was nearly hoarse. Suddenly, as if by magic, two little Indians and a white dog appeared on the back porch. They were wide-eyed and puzzled about all the fuss being made. Lady barked and jumped about, adding a little of her own happy spirit to the excitement.

"Where have you been, and why didn't you answer when I called? Didn't you hear the car horn tooting?" Mrs. Grant asked in crisp tones.

44

"We went walking," said Singing Tree. "We wanted to see the bears and mountain lions that you said might be in the woods to hurt us. We didn't see any mountain lions or bears, so it's all right to go into the woods by ourselves. You don't have to worry now, Mamma. Honest. There are no big things to eat us, you see."

Mrs. Grant looked helplessly to her husband. "Tell them, will you?" she pleaded.

"You may not have found any wild animals there today," Mr. Grant warned, "but you just didn't happen to be where they were this evening. Perhaps if you went another time they would be there, and they could easily pounce on you, hurting terribly; they might even *kill* you!"

Mrs. Grant said, "I am not like Mrs. Mahoney, giving you lots of chances. I must spank you for what you have done so that you will understand and remember that it is really important for you to do as you are told."

The children's eyes grew enormous. How could their kind new mother do such a cruel thing as to spank them?

Mrs. Grant took a ping-pong paddle from a kitchen drawer and led the girls to their room, where she administered it soundly.

"I am very sorry I had to do that," Mrs. Grant said while the girls sputtered and sobbed, "but you were the ones who made me do it, you know. I want you to be good Indians; the best Indians in the world!"

She walked out and closed the door gently behind her as even louder crying burst from the girls. Finally that stopped, and then the family in the living room could hear the tinkling tunes of the music boxes, playing over and over until they all began to feel dizzy.

Mrs. Grant was sitting at the kitchen table reading the newspaper when she heard softly padding footsteps. Thinking it would be Singing Tree coming to her, she was surprised to see Laughing Water walk through the door instead. She was *really* surprised to see Laughing Water smiling and most surprised when Laughing Water climbed up on her lap and hugged her.

Mrs. Grant hugged the little Indian tight. She had hoped many weeks for this moment. Presently Laughing Water said to her, "You love us, don't you, Mamma?"

"Yes, I do," answered Mrs. Grant. "How did you find that out?" "Because you paddled us hard," Laughing Water replied. "You want us to remember to be good so we will grow up to be good Indians. That means you care about us; so that means you love us!"

Soon Singing Tree came padding softly across the floor and tried to share her new mother's lap with Laughing Water. Mrs. Grant rocked them both back and forth and sang, "Wawatisi, my papoose, close your coal-black eyes—"

When the song was finished she led them to bed. For the first time the little Indians wanted to kiss their mother and father good-night.

Singing Tree said happily, "Mamma and Daddy love us, and Jesus loves us; so I guess everything is splenidford."

"More like splendid," said Mrs. Grant, smiling as she switched off the light.

46

Chapter 6

Ketchup Races and the Blue Bow

One day Mrs. Grant allowed Laughing Water and Singing Tree to eat their supper before the rest of the family came home. The girls had complained so long about being hungry that she finally gave them their meal just to have some peace. As they were eating, Singing Tree asked, "Mamma, do you know what ketchup races are?"

"Dear me, no!" exclaimed Mrs. Grant. "I haven't heard of such a thing! What will I be hearing next?"

"I'll tell you about ketchup races," Singing Tree said with a happy smile. "Ketchup races are games that you try to see which bottle of ketchup can get emptied first. It's a kind of slick game, isn't it?"

Mrs. Grant laughed. "A very slick game, I'd say, but please don't empty a whole bottle of ketchup on one patty just to see who can empty a bottle first!"

Mrs. Grant ironed clothes as she talked to the girls and waited for the others to come home. "Tell us a story as you iron. Please, Mamma," Laughing Water begged when she had finished eating.

"Another story about old-fashioned Indians," chimed in Singing Tree. "Those old-fashioned Indians were good Indians—not like the bad Indians on Mrs. Mahoney's television."

"See what the time is, Singing Tree," said Mrs. Grant, "and then I'll know if there is time to tell you a story before Daddy comes home. Tell Mamma what the big hand is on and what the little hand is on."

Every day Mrs. Grant had been trying to teach Singing Tree to count and to say her ABC's, but Singing Tree always felt much more interested in playing with Lady and the calves or getting into interesting mischief; learning was hard work!

47

Now Singing Tree ran to the kitchen to look at the copper wall clock shaped like a skillet. "What does the clock say?" Mrs. Grant called from the utility room.

"It says," Singing Tree began. Then she paused. "Now let me see! Oh, yes, the short hand is up top and the big hand is on B!"

"On B?" Mrs. Grant groaned, wondering what had become of her hours of hard work.

"That's all right," Singing Tree said, "that means there's twenty hours for you to tell us an old-fashioned Indian story."

"All right," Mrs. Grant agreed, "maybe there'll be time to tell you a little something about the Plains Indians. You will remember that Jamey told you the Plains Indians lived in tepees. One of the reasons they lived in tepees was that they were great buffalo hunters. They used buffalo meat for food and the hides to make clothes and tepees. Since the buffalo roamed all over the Plains, the Indians moved their homes often as they went in search of the herds. Because the tepees were like tents, the Indians could take them down and move them easily and then put them up when they came to a good hunting ground."

"That was a good idea, Mamma," said Laughing Water. "They couldn't move brick houses, could they?"

"That's right," agreed Mrs. Grant. "One thing true of the Indians everywhere," she added, "was that they did the best they could with what they had. Those Plains Indians used every part of the buffalo. They made blankets and robes to keep themselves warm in the cold winters; they made glue from the hooves; the horns and bones were used to make decorations for clothing. When the white people came, many of them wasted parts of the buffalo, and this upset the Indians. They could not understand the white man's wasteful ways."

"Was there a lot of snow in the winter?" asked Singing Tree. "If there was, I don't think the Indians could go through the deep snow to chase buffalo."

"The Plains Indians and the coastal Indians both had ways of preserving their food so they would not have to do much hunting in the winter," Mrs. Grant said. "The coastal Indians dried their fish by smoking it over fires. The plains Indians cut the buffalo

48

meat into thin strips and dried it in the sun and smoked it over their fires. Doing that was called 'jerking' the meat. When the white people came west, they learned to do that too. The Plains Indians ground their dried meat just as the Zuñi Indian women ground their wheat and corn to make bread. When the dried meat was powdery, the Indians mixed it with melted fat and with dried, ground berries to make a winter food that was called 'pemmican.' This was good food for the Indians to take with them on long trips; it kept a long time, and it was much lighter to carry than the big loads of buffalo meat necessary to feed a large family. It could be eaten without stopping to cook it."

"What did the little Plains Indian girls do, Mamma? The ones as big as Singing Tree and me?"

"I think they learned to help in all the things their mothers did," Mrs. Grant answered. "The mothers made tepees or mended them when they were torn; they gathered firewood and carried fresh water to the camps. Food had to be prepared. The buffalo hides had to be worked on. And there were clothes and moccasins to be made for all the family. I'm sure it all made a lot of hard work for the Indian mothers and that they needed the help of their girls."

"If I could be an old-fashioned Indian, I would make some moccasins for Jamey," said Singing Tree.

"I hear the car!" exclaimed Laughing Water, and the two rushed out to greet the rest of the family.

Every school day, now, Singing Tree ran down the hill to meet the bus when it brought Laughing Water home from school.

"Hello, there, who's this waiting to catch the bus when it is really coming-home time and not going-to-school time?" Mr. Sam would say. "I think I see a little Indian who slept too long and missed the bus this morning! Sleepyhead!"

"No, I was up early, Mr. Sam!" Singing Tree would protest. "I don't want to catch the bus to go to school. I'm not old enough to go to school yet. I just want to ride to the bus turnaround with the other big kids."

"Hop in, then, little Indian, and we'll see what we can do for you," Mr. Sam would say.

49

One day Singing Tree left to meet the bus before it was time. Her face and dress were spattered from mud-pie making, but that did not bother Singing Tree. Her bus ride was all that mattered. Mrs. Grant felt embarrassed when she found what Singing Tree had done.

The next afternoon she made sure that she watched Singing Tree closely. Some time after lunch she called Singing Tree inside, scrubbed her shiny clean, and dressed her in a clean sun dress. "Promise Mamma you won't ever leave the house again looking like you did yesterday. No one likes to see dirty children riding on the school bus."

"I went 'cause I was afraid I'd miss the ride," Singing Tree explained, "but I won't do it anymore, Mamma. I promise. If I don't get down to the bus on time, that will be my own tough luck, won't it, Mamma?"

Later in the afternoon, when the girls were tidying their room, Laughing Water began to squeal in excitement. "Mamma, come quickly! The baby birds have come out. I can hear their mother talking to them, and they are answering in squeaky little voices."

When Mrs. Grant got to the room, Laughing Water was leaning out the window looking at the nest in the tree. Laughing Water's report was correct, and Mother and Father Kingbird turned out to be very noisy parents, just as they had been fussy and noisy nest builders. They talked and scolded each other and the babies. They were also busy parents, swooping down on every moth and grub that came into view and carrying them back to their hungry babies in the nest.

When Jamey came home, he wanted to climb the oak tree to see how many eggs had hatched and what the new babies looked like. He waited until the parents were gone from the nest to make his climb and was almost to the top of the tree where the nest swayed in the breeze when Mrs. Kingbird returned. She darted at Jamey's head, pecking angrily at him; she screeched in bird language and beat her wings wildly.

The mother bird did not really scare Jamey, for she was too small to hurt him; but he climbed down because he did not want

50

to worry her. Then Mrs. Kingbird followed him and pecked at him until he was close to the kitchen porch. When her husband returned with a large moth in his beak, she seemed to be telling him with shrill cries about the threat that had come to their nest.

The girls continued watching the birds, and soon a big hawk swooped down over the kingbirds' home. It became plain that Mrs. Kingbird did not like hawks any more than she liked boys. She sailed off after the hawk using all the harsh bird words she could remember. After she had chased him safely over the eastern hills, she came back to her squeaking children.

That night as the girls went to sleep they could hear the bird family talking softly and drowsily to each other.

"It must be nice to be a little bird," said Laughing Water to Singing Tree, "all those soft rags under you, and a nice warm-feathered mamma to sit on you and keep you warm! I think I'd like to be a baby bird much more than I'd like to be an old-fashioned Indian child."

Laughing Water came in one afternoon all hot and tired from walking up the hill from the bus. Mrs. Grant felt so sorry for her that she left what she was doing to help her undress and put on her play clothes. She gave her an applesauce cookie and a glass of cold milk; then she rocked the little Indian on her lap until she stopped feeling miserable.

"I brought home a present for you yesterday, Mamma," Laughing Water said shyly. "I hid it in my room. I was going to keep it for you until your birthday, but I want to give it to you now."

"I will close my eyes until you bring it to me," Mrs. Grant promised. "That way it will be a big surprise."

Laughing Water soon scrambled back up on Mrs. Grant's lap. "Now you can open your eyes, Mamma," she said.

Mrs. Grant opened her eyes and took a large green envelope from Laughing Water's hand. She found a big green card inside. On the front of the card, edged with white lace from a paper doily, was a picture of Laughing Water; below the picture Laughing Water had printed "Happy Birthday!"

Mrs. Grant smiled, and then she opened the card. In Laughing

51

Water's printing she read, "I love you, Mother."

"That is a lovely birthday present," she said, hugging the little Indian close. "That makes Mamma very, very happy!"

Hurriedly putting down Laughing Water she said, "Oh, dear! I had forgotten to keep an eye on Singing Tree while I was talking to you. Everything is terribly quiet. Where did she go?"

"I didn't see where she went," said Laughing Water. "I haven't seen her since she came in from the school bus."

They called Singing Tree. They went through all the rooms calling her name. They looked in the barn and the calf shed.

"I hear Lady barking in the woods," said Laughing Water. "Do you think she would be with Singing Tree?"

"Just wait until I get my walking shoes, and we shall go and see," said Mrs. Grant.

As the two went deeper and deeper into the woods they called and called. "Oh, dear! Where can she be?" sighed Mrs. Grant. "I wonder what she can possibly be up to this time. I hope it is nothing too bad or too dangerous. I think she has done about every naughty thing she could think of already."

"Mrs. Mahoney always spanked Singing Tree for getting into mischief," suggested Laughing Water. "Maybe if you spank her she'll stop getting into mischief."

"No, I don't think she would be helped by my spanking her every time she was in mischief," Mrs. Grant said. "She is looking for interesting things to do all the time. I don't think she means to be naughty. The things she does are fun to her, and they give her something to think about. You go to school all day and have interesting things to do and other nice children to play with. Singing Tree has none of that. I think when she goes to school she will stop getting into mischief."

Lady came bounding from a clump of manzanitas. She barked and yapped and jumped all over Laughing Water, licking her face and hands.

"Singing Tree, where are you?" called Mrs. Grant. Seeing Lady there, she could guess that Singing Tree was not very far away. A soft, rustling sound came from the bushes where Lady had been; then up popped Singing Tree, carrying the big blue bow for

52

shooting arrows which usually stood in the corner of Jamey's room. From the time Laughing Water and Singing Tree had come to live with the Grants, Singing Tree had longed to get hold of that big blue bow. Her chance to slip into Jamey's room unnoticed came when Mrs. Grant was comforting Laughing Water in the kitchen. She had crept, with the big bow, down the basement stairs and out the basement door into the woods.

"Singing Tree!" said Mrs. Grant with firm lips and a displeased expression. "Jamey will be very angry if he comes home to find that you have been in his room and taken his bow! How many, many times have I told you *not* to touch things that don't belong to you?"

Singing Tree did not look at all worried or ashamed.

"What's a bow, Mamma?" Her black eyes looked wide with innocence. "Is this big blue thing a bow?"

"Yes, it is a bow," said Mrs. Grant. "Daddy gave it to Jamey for Christmas, and Jamey treasures it very much. He loves to go into the woods to shoot arrows from it. You were a very naughty girl to go into Jamey's room!"

"What's arrows, Mamma?" Singing Tree asked, still not impressed with Mrs. Grant's lecture.

Mrs. Grant sat on a large hollow log and sighed. "What am I to do with this wild little Indian? Will she ever take any notice of anything I try to teach her?"

Laughing Water sat on the log beside Mrs. Grant.

Singing Tree threw down the bow and jumped into Mrs. Grant's lap. She put her arms around Mrs. Grant's neck and gave her a big, smacking kiss.

"You know why I like to kiss you, Mamma?" asked Singing Tree.

"I wouldn't have any idea," Mrs. Grant answered.

"I like to kiss you because your cheek is so soft and it smells decerious!"

"Decerious?" asked Mrs. Grant and Laughing Water at the same moment.

"I think you mean delicious," Mrs. Grant said, biting her lip, trying not to laugh, but smiling despite herself.

"An arrow," she said, "is a thing you shoot from a bow like this.

53

It is a long, pointed stick, and when it is shot from the bow it sticks into whatever it hits. If you ask Jamey to bring out his bow and arrow after supper I'm sure he'll show you how they work. I suppose every good Indian should know how bows and arrows work."

"Why?" both little Indians asked.

"Why?" repeated Mrs. Grant. "Because years ago old-fashioned Indians used bows and arrows for hunting. The woods Indians were great bow-and-arrow Indians."

"Were they afraid in the big dark woods?" asked Singing Tree. "Did they make houses, or did they live under the trees?"

"Oh, they made houses," Mrs. Grant replied, "and they called them wigwams or long houses. The wigwams had frames that were round instead of pointed like the tepees, and they usually covered them with bark instead of buffalo skins. The woods Indians ate some vegetables and some fish, but they mostly lived on deer they shot with their bows and arrows. They used every part of the deer, never wasting anything, just as the plains Indians never wasted any part of the buffalo. But in one way the woods Indians did not do very well. Instead of sharing, like the Zuñi Indians did, different tribes or families fought with each other about their hunting grounds. So, by not learning to share, they caused themselves a lot of trouble.

"Is sharing the bestest thing for good Indians to do, Mamma?" asked Singing Tree.

"It is the best thing for everyone to do," Mrs. Grant said. "When Jesus was here living on the earth, he taught His followers to share. There are many ways we can share, and when we love Jesus He shows us how we can share at different times. Sometimes we might see a little child who badly needs clothing, and we can help by giving some of ours; or if we know someone doesn't have very much to eat, we can share our food. We share when we put money in the offering at church, because the money buys food and supplies for God's workers. It also buys things little children need in far-off places. It helps to build schools and hospitals for people who do not have enough money to build their own. It helps to buy medicines for poor sick people."

"The teacher said we give our money to Jesus," said Laughing Water.

"The Bible tells us that if we share with those who need us to help them we are acting the same as if we were really doing all these things for Jesus Himself," Mrs. Grant explained. "Loving to share shows that we truly love Jesus," she added.

Mrs. Grant lifted Singing Tree from her lap to the ground and stood up.

"Everyone will be home soon," she said. "Let's put Jamey's bow back where it belongs; and remember, Singing Tree, you are not to go into Jamey's room again unless he invites you. And you are not to touch things which belong to other people. Do you understand?"

"Yes, Mamma, I'll redember not to go into Jamey's room," promised Singing Tree. "And I'll redember not to touch other people's things a longest time. I'll redember until tomorrow."

Chapter 7

A Ghost in the Closet

One bright happy morning a long envelope, the first mail that Singing Tree had ever received, was waiting for her in the letter box near the school-bus stop. She gurgled and yelled and sprang about like a young deer jumping the pasture fence with Lady on its heels.

"Tell me what it says, Mamma! Tell me, quick! I'm all ber-cited!" she cried.

"Excited is the word, you know," Mrs. Grant said while she waited for Singing Tree to open the envelope. Singing Tree pulled out a typewritten sheet of paper and handed it to her.

"Hmmmmm!" Mrs. Grant said, and then smiled. "It says that you are invited to go to school to visit the first-grade room so that you can find out what it will be like when you start school."

"Goody! Goody! Goody!" Singing Tree yelled. Lady jumped around her and barked to show that she shared the moment of great excitement.

Singing Tree gave Mrs. Grant no peace for the next several days. What dress would she wear on her first day at school? What socks would match the dress? Would she wear her good shoes or her tennis shoes or her sandals? Mrs. Grant grew dizzy trying to answer the questions as fast as Singing Tree could ask them.

"Is this the day?" Singing Tree asked every morning at the crack of dawn.

"Not today," Mrs. Grant would say, but finally the day did come when Mrs. Grant drove Singing Tree to school and left her there to have a wonderful time looking at books, coloring, playing with other children on swings and slides, and talking to the first-grade teacher. Singing Tree had fun with all this, but she liked best the milk and cookies which the teacher served just before Mrs. Grant arrived to take her home.

That night Mr. Grant said, "Well, Singing Tree, how did you like school?"

"It was all right," Singing Tree said without looking up from the doll dress which Celia was teaching her to sew.

"All right!" exclaimed Mr. Grant. "I thought you'd be so excited about school you wouldn't be able to wait for September to roll around! What's the matter with our little Indian?"

"I've desrideded that I don't want to go to school," she answered, her mouth drooping at the corners. "All you do every morning is get up and rush around and you're tired because you don't get enough sleep."

"The answer to that big problem is for you to go to bed much earlier than you usually do," Mr. Grant suggested. "Then you won't be tired at school."

"I don't want to go to school, Daddy. Honest, I don't!" Singing Tree moaned, tears appearing in her eyes. "Mamma will be too lonely if I go away and leave her; she needs someone to look after her, and a good Indian is the best baby-sitter for Mamma!"

Mr. Grant put his arm around Singing Tree. "You're tired from such a big day and so much excitement," he said. "You'll feel better tomorrow, and you needn't worry about Mamma. Lady and the calves will take care of her while you're at school."

A few days later, school let out for the summer, and Laughing Water could stay at home every day to play with Singing Tree. Laughing Water was excited because she had done well at school and would be going into the second grade when school started again. Her teacher had given her a good-citizen ribbon, and she felt very proud of that.

Big brother Richard came home from college. He gave the girls airplane rides by taking each of them by a hand and foot and whirling them around the living room.

And a few days later Celia graduated from high school. The day of her graduation she stood on the sidewalk near the front steps for her picture to be taken. She wore a royal-blue robe and

57

cap, and from her cap hung a yellow tassle which, she explained to the girls, she had received because she had worked hard and received good grades.

"If you work hard and behave like good Indians should, you will have gold tassles to wear someday," promised Celia.

"I want to be a graderatishon Indian," chirped Singing Tree. "I want big blue things swinging in the wind, and I want pretty yellow things hanging down!"

"Er—" said Jamey, clearing his throat. "I think the word is graduation, and you can't be a graduation Indian for another twelve years. Tough luck, I'd say. There'll be a lot of work between now and then. Anyway, let's get Celia's graduation over first."

"Oh, Mamma!" cried Singing Tree, having already forgotten Jamey's speech. "Are you going to wear those low-down up heels to Celia's graderatishon? Pretty, pretty pink low-down up heels. I wish I could wear them!"

The Grant family crowded into the bleacher seats of the school stadium between families and friends of the other graduating students. They had arrived early enough to get seats near the aisle where Celia would march in and out of the stadium. When the humming and buzzing of the excited people had stopped and everyone was waiting quietly for the band to play the first notes of the graduation march, a big, plump woman in a bright yellow-green dress walked along the aisle near the Grants, searching for a seat. In a startled voice loud enough for hundreds of people to hear, Singing Tree called out, "Ha, ha! Look, Mamma! Look!" She clapped her hands wildly. I see someone who's awful fat!"

Mrs. Grant's face grew about as red as the beets she had served with salad for supper as people for many rows around giggled and tittered. She leaned over to her husband and Jamey and said in a soft voice, "Right now, I could really do with those walking shoes! I'd like to vanish like lightning!"

When Singing Tree's lips opened to say "Look!" the second time Mrs. Grant clapped a gloved hand over her mouth and put a finger to her own mouth, saying "Sh!" and was most relieved to hear the band swell into the march.

58

When the band began to play "Battle Hymn of the Republic," the audience was still and quiet. When the part came which says, "In the beauty of the lilies Christ was born across the sea, with the glory in His bosom that transfigures you and me," the last rays of a glorious evening sunset shone through the tears that filled Mrs. Grant's eyes and trickled down her cheeks; she felt touched by the loveliness of the music, by the meaning of the words which she had known for many years, and by the sudden realization that her oldest daughter had grown up. Many others in the audience also dabbed with handkerchiefs at tear-filled eyes.

Then, suddenly, without any warning, Singing Tree said in a voice loud enough to be heard above trumpets and cymbals of the band: "Mamma, have we ate, yet? I'm *hungry!*"

"Oh, *no!*" whispered Mrs. Grant, covering her face with her hands.

"I'm afraid it's 'Oh, yes!'" Jamey leaned over to whisper, his face also a little pink as some of his friends giggled in seats behind them.

Singing Tree, sitting between Mrs. Grant and Jamey, looked from one face to the other with a wide-eyed frown that seemed to say, "What have I done wrong now?"

On the way home, when all the music, marching, talking, handshakes, kisses, and present-giving had ended, Mrs. Grant delivered just another in her series of lectures. But this one she gave with special sternness. It was called WHAT NOT TO DO AND SAY IN PUBLIC PLACES!

Excitement came in many ways that summer—like the day that Mrs. Kingbird brought out her babies to teach them to fly. Laughing Water and Singing Tree spent almost the whole day watching and many hours of the days that followed. The baby birds first learned to glide; then they began flapping their tiny wings. They learned to circle the oak trees a dozen times without stopping; they learned to duck and dive and twist and squirm in midair; they learned to get back on the wing each time they made a forced landing. Singing Tree and Laughing Water also watched the mother bird catch food for her noisy children whenever she

59

could spare time from the flying lessons. They heard her scold and shriek at her babies when they did not please her. And at night when the girls climbed into their beds, they heard the babies talking together in the oak trees outside their open window.

On another exciting morning the whole family piled into Mr. Grant's car and headed for the ocean. The little Indians had never seen the sea. When they first saw the foamy waves and heard them boom and thunder, they danced and squealed and held their ears. They splashed their feet in the shallow water and then let little waves chase them back up the beach. They begged for permission to run into the big waves and get wet, but everybody shook their heads and said the day was too cool. They settled for searching with Jamey and Richard for shells and pink and yellow starfish in the water holes of the gray rocks that piled up along the shore. They poked a fat stick against the middle of a sea anemone and watched it close its lacy tentacles around the stick. Then they joined the rest of the family in a gay run along the beach, feeling the spray on their faces, until their cheeks glowed rose-red and they were so out of breath they could run no longer. Finally they curled up by the campfire, wrapped in light wool blankets, and watched Mrs. Grant and Celia cook potatoes and eggs in an iron skillet over the fire for lunch.

After lunch they discovered smooth grayish-white sea-gull feathers lying on the beach. When Mrs. Grant told them that some of the old-fashioned Indians made headdresses with feathers, the two little Indians thought they had found real treasures.

"Not particularly from sea-gull feathers," Mrs. Grant explained, "but usually from eagle feathers."

"Each feather in an Indian's headdress meant that he had done some brave deed to deserve it," she said. "Sometime you will probably hear someone say, 'That's a feather in your cap!' and you will understand it to mean that you have done something very well or very special."

At home the next day Mrs. Grant found some corrugated cardboard from a carton and showed the girls how she used to make Indian headdresses with cardboard and dyed chicken feathers. Mrs. Grant cut the cardboard into two strips, each about two inches wide and long enough to go around the girls' heads. She bent each cardboard strip into a circle and joined the ends with a piece of elastic which she sewed to the cardboard with needle and thread.

"OK," Mrs. Grant said, "these bands will fit around your heads with the elastic in the back. Now bring me those sea-gull feathers you picked up yesterday."

The girls returned with the feathers and watched with open mouths and wide eyes as Mrs. Grant dipped some of the grayish feathers into a bowl of dark liquid and they came out red. She dipped the rest of the feathers into another bowl, and they came out yellow.

"What is that stuff?" Singing Tree asked.

Mrs. Grant smiled. "We've always called it Easter-egg dye. When Jamey and Celia were small, they would use it to color hard-boiled eggs at Easter time."

Then Mrs. Grant began to stick the stems of the feathers into the little tunnels made by the corrugation on the cardboard headbands, first a red feather, then a yellow feather, a red one and a yellow one, until a bright feather stuck up from every little tunnel.

Mrs. Grant fitted the headdresses onto the girls' heads, pushing them down snugly so the front of the bands circled their foreheads. The girls flew up the steps to their bedrooms to gaze into their mirror.

"Now we are feather-head Indians," cried Singing Tree joyfully. "That's just what I wanted to be; a feather-head Indian!"

For the next several days Mrs. Grant could glance out the windows almost anytime and find two wild befeathered Indians racing through the fields.

One night after the girls had gone to bed, Mrs. Grant noticed that the music boxes played an unusually long time. When the music finally stopped, she could hear loud sobs coming from the girls' room.

"What now?" Mrs. Grant said to her husband.

Mrs. Grant snapped on the bedroom light and found Singing Tree crouched in her bed, the blankets pulled over her head.

61

"Whatever is it now?" she asked.

"There's something in the closet, Mamma," the little girl cried.

"Something? What kind of something?" Mrs. Grant sounded surprised.

"It's a ghost," wailed Singing Tree. "A big, horrible, breathy ghost!"

"Did you see it?" asked Mrs. Grant.

"No, but I know it's there because the girls at Mrs. Mahoney's place told me that there is a ghost in every closet. There was one in our bedroom at Mrs. Mahoney's place, wasn't there, Laughing Water?"

All this time Laughing Water had been sitting up in bed, her face very pale and tears glistening on her cheeks. Her voice came out small and trembly when she said, "Yes, Mamma, that's right."

"I shall look in the closet," Mrs. Grant said, and she drew back the sliding doors. "As a matter of fact, I cleaned out this closet a few days ago. All I saw was too many clothes and far too many toys and far too much untidiness."

Both the girls stared with terrified eyes as Mrs. Grant put her hands into the closet and pushed back the dozens of dresses of every pretty color and style. Then she stepped inside the closet.

"Don't, Mamma!" Singing Tree bellowed. "The ghost will get you, and we'll have no sweet Mamma!"

"Where are you, ghost?" Mrs. Grant asked. "Come out and show yourself to me!"

She took out all of the clothing and toys, piling them on the foot of the girls' beds.

Taking the little girls' hands, she led them into the closet where they found nothing but emptiness. She hugged the girls close.

"Have you forgotten what Mamma told you about the kind Father in heaven who loves us and cares for us, and especially for His little children? Believe me when I tell you there is not such a thing as a ghost, and I think it was very naughty of the big girls at Mrs. Mahoney's place to frighten you by telling you there are ghosts in every closet. They were getting fun out of seeing how afraid they could make you. Won't you remember that our kind Father is watching over us always and His helpers, the angels, are with you when you are awake or when you are asleep? Will you promise Mamma you will remember?"

The children nodded thoughtfully and crawled back into bed. Mrs. Grant sat on the edge of Singing Tree's bed and sang for them the song they loved so much: "Jesus loves me, this I know; for the Bible tells me so."

When she had finished singing the girls were smiling.

"Will you—" Laughing Water hesitated. "Well, will you say prayers with us tonight, Mamma?"

"Of course I will," Mrs. Grant replied. The girls knelt, one on each side of their mother, and she taught them a little prayer:

> "Jesus, tender Shepherd, hear me;
> Bless Thy little lamb tonight.
> Through the darkness be Thou near me;
> Keep me safe till morning light."

"Am I Jesus' little lamb?" Singing Tree asked with a happy lilt to her voice.

"Yes, you are, and so is Laughing Water. Jesus is the good and loving Shepherd, and He does not want any of His little lambs to be hurt."

Back into bed the children climbed, and Laughing Water said, "Mamma, we don't want to make our music boxes go tonight. They can't help us to be safe, like I thought. Jesus is the One who keeps us safe, and we want to say prayers with you every night."

Chapter 8

The Runaway

"Did you have a nice sleep last night?" Mrs. Grant asked the girls when they awoke.

"Oh, yes, Mamma," replied Singing Tree. "The ghosts didn't come, but the angels did. Laughing Water knows they came, because she said she woke up and saw the angels over our beds. There was a pretty white light in the room."

Mrs. Grant said, "You won't worry about ghosts anymore, will you? Believing there are ghosts in closets is really very silly. You know, the old-fashioned Indians, before anyone taught them about Jesus, believed that there were ghosts everywhere and that the ghosts caused people to be sick and made bad weather so the crops would not grow."

"That was pretty silly," said Laughing Water.

"They were what we call 'superstitious,'" Mrs. Grant told the girls. "They believed things without any good or sensible reason. Believing that there are ghosts about to frighten little children is also being superstitious. Today we know that sickness and death are many times caused by germs entering our bodies. Sometimes we get sick because we don't take good care of ourselves by eating good foods and getting plenty of rest and exercise. When our bodies break down, it is quite often our own doing and not the workings of some ghostly spirits."

The girls were playing with their feather headdresses, Celia was sewing, Jamey and Richard were helping Mr. Grant in the vegetable garden, and Mrs. Grant was ironing, trying to get all the clothes ironed and in the closets before the day grew too hot.

"Did the little old-fashioned Indians ever get stories told them,

64

Mamma?" asked Singing Tree, who was always not quite satisfied with doing one thing unless she was planning ahead to two or three other activities.

"What was the idea in bringing that up?" Mrs. Grant asked with a chuckle.

"I just thought maybe little old-fashioned Indians liked stories like this little Indian does," said Singing Tree. "Did you ever hear any stories that little Indian children would like to know about, Mamma?"

"I'm sure I have heard a number of Indian stories," said Mrs. Grant. "Do you think there are any Indians living around here who might like to hear an Indian story?"

"I think there might be two," said Singing Tree.

"All right," Mrs. Grant said as her iron slid back and forth across Mr. Grant's white shirt. "I know a good story about a little Indian boy who wanted very, very much to go hunting with the men and the big boys, but he was far too young. He kept asking and asking his father, who was chief of the tribe, if he might go. At last his father grew tired of his asking, so he said, 'All right, my son, when you have brought me a feather from the tail of a fierce bald eagle, then I will let you go on the hunt.'

"The boy slipped away from camp and looked many days for a bald eagle. At last he found a mother eagle crippled because someone had shot an arrow through her wing. Her poor babies were starving because she could not fly away to catch food for them to eat.

" 'I must feed those babies,' the boy said. 'They are beautiful babies, and it will break their mother's heart to see them die because she cannot get food for them.' So he searched about and found the food the babies needed. Trying very patiently, he coaxed the babies and the mother to eat, even though they were afraid of him. The birds and the Indian boy became great friends. When the mother was well and able to care for her babies again, the boy left for home. He carried with him a large feather from the eagle's tail.

" 'My father will not know how easy it was for me to get this feather,' he kept telling himself. 'He will think I was strong and

65

brave to be able to get close enough to a fierce eagle to get her tail feather.'

"By the time the boy reached home he felt troubled, because he realized that what he had wanted his father to believe was really a lie. When his father called him, he said, 'Father, at first I wanted you to believe that it was very hard work for me to bring back this feather to you, but I cannot tell a lie. It was very easy for me to get the feather, for the mother eagle had been crippled by an arrow in her wing and she was unable to get away from me. I fed her babies with rabbit and I took care of her until she was well. By the time she was well she knew me as a friend, so it was easy for me to take the feather from her tail. I cannot go on the hunt, for it took no bravery for me to bring you this feather.'

"The chief was very quiet as he sat and thought of what his boy had told him. For a long time he sat; then he said, 'My son, I want you to go on the hunt. You have shown me that you are a real man. You were patient and kind to a fierce enemy. *It is much harder to be kind to your enemy than to fight him.* You have shown your father a great lesson. You may go on the hunt, my son, and you have my rich blessing.' "

"That was a very good story," said Laughing Water.

"He was a good Indian to take care of the poor birds," said Singing Tree.

Then the girls turned their attention to their headdresses with renewed interest, and pretended to be caring for a family of fierce eagles.

Soon Singing Tree was wrestling on the back lawn with Lady. "What's going on here?" asked Mr. Grant, watching with a smile.

"Lady and Singing Tree are wrestling, Daddy," puffed Singing Tree, "and I'm coming out ahead, Daddy! I'm really coming out ahead!"

Mrs. Grant went into the girls' room to put away their freshly ironed clothes, and a horrible mess of rumpled clothes and toys awaited her. Soon she was calling the girls.

"I cannot understand how two small girls can make a room

so terribly untidy!" she scolded. "I have never seen such a mess in all my life! There will be no lunch for you until this room is shipshape!"

Both the girls were practically tripping over their lips, they were so angry about having been called from their play. After a few minutes of the tidying business Singing Tree came to Mrs. Grant and said, "I don't like living here, Mamma. I never had to tidy my room at Mrs. Mahoney's house. I'm going to run away! I'll go to a house where the mother doesn't make little kids work! I'll throw things everywhere and it won't matter. I think I'll go back to Mrs. Mahoney's place!"

"This IS a surprise!" exclaimed Mrs. Grant. "How do you plan to get to Mrs. Mahoney's place? She lives a long, long way over the mountains from here—almost a hundred miles, as a matter of fact. How do you plan to travel all that way?"

"I'll walk," said Singing Tree. "With these strong Indian legs, I'll walk!"

"Do you plan to take a suitcase with you?"

"Oh, yes, Mamma," said Singing Tree, brightening at the thought. "A suitcase with all my clothes in it."

Mrs. Grant borrowed a suitcase from Richard—the largest one he had brought home from college—and took it to the girls' bedroom.

"Here," she said, opening it on the bed. "Make sure you put in everything you need for the long trip, won't you?"

She helped Singing Tree pack many of her dresses and shoes, and the suitcase filled up with amazing speed.

"What about some toys to play with?" suggested Mrs. Grant. "Do you think there will be time to play along the way?"

"Oh, yes, Mamma," replied Singing Tree. "I must have toys!"

She jammed into the case a stuffed Scottie dog and a large green caterpillar which was as long as the suitcase.

"I don't think the music box will squeeze in," Singing Tree said a little wistfully, "but never mind, Mamma, I can say prayers instead of listening to the music if I want to go to sleep."

"Where will you sleep?" Mrs. Grant asked.

"In some house or under the trees," Singing Tree said. "I

67

wouldn't need to take blankets, because it is too hot every night in bed. I think I'd better be going now."

"Kiss me good-bye," said Mrs. Grant, putting her arms around the little Indian, "and be sure to say good-bye to Daddy and the others." Kissing the child, she said, "Write to us sometime and let us know how you are. We'll be wondering about you and missing you."

The good-byes were all said, and Singing Tree started down the drive, dragging the suitcase on the gravel. It weighed too much for her to get it off the ground.

"That isn't the best treatment for a suitcase," said Mr. Grant, looking rather anxious.

"She won't get very far," Jamey smiled. "Anyone that can't get his luggage off the ground doesn't stand much chance of reaching his destination."

Singing Tree turned back to wave to her family with almost every step she took. Halfway down the long drive she stopped and opened the suitcase.

"Whatever is she doing now?" asked Celia.

The question was soon answered: Singing Tree had decided to take off her boots and put on her good socks and shoes—the ones that were kept for special times like going to church. She had quite a struggle with the buckles, but finally she was on the way again, dragging the suitcase inch by inch. Tiring, she sat in the long grass.

"I think I'll go down and have a talk with her and see why she is resting so long," Mrs. Grant said. "She must be having troubles."

"Why are you sitting here wasting time?" Mrs. Grant asked. "You have such a long way to go you'll never get there before dark if you don't go right away."

"I'm going to have fun," said Singing Tree. "I was just sitting here thinking about all the things I will do and the nice things I will eat."

"Oh, what do you plan to have for lunch?" asked Mrs. Grant.

"I'll go to Billing's Market," she chirped, "and I'll buy the biggest ice cream I ever had. You won't be there to say that too much ice cream is bad for girls, will you? It will be fun to fill up on ice cream, Mamma!"

"How will you get the ice cream?" Mrs. Grant asked.

"I'll get it from Mr. Billing," Singing Tree stated.

"Do you have any money to give him for the ice cream?"

Singing Tree grew very quiet. Tears started popping out on her cheeks.

"I spended my money that you gave me, Mamma," she said. "I spended it all and took some to church."

"Do you think you are big enough to take care of yourself on the long trip?" asked Mrs. Grant.

"I think I'll come home and unpack my suitcase," sniffed Singing Tree. "I don't think I could carry that suitcase all the way to Mrs. Mahoney's place." She stood up and put her hand in Mrs. Grant's. "Mamma, I don't think it was a very good idea to go away from home," she said. "I think I'll go home and clean up my messy room."

After the girls had tidied their room and eaten lunch, Mrs. Grant asked them to walk down the hill to the mailbox and get the mail. When they returned, Singing Tree said, "Lady went with us, Mamma, and you know what she did? She chased those snarly, sabbage dogs of Mr. Rippon so we could pretent they weren't going to try to eat us. And you know what Lady thought? She thought she was going to get a dog bone in the mail. She was very disinported!"

"I think you mean that Lady was disappointed," suggested Mrs. Grant. "What do you have in your mouth?"

"Just a green nut thing," said Singing Tree. "Laughing Water has one in her mouth too."

Laughing Water showed her "green nut thing" to her mother. "They are acorns," Mrs. Grant told the girls. "Acorns, when planted, grow into baby oak trees that grow into big oak trees like the one near the kitchen window."

"Are the acorns good to eat?" Laughing Water asked, rolling the green acorn around in her mouth.

"They are hard and bitter," Mrs. Grant said, "but those of the old-fashioned Indians who were seed gatherers found a way to

69

make the acorns good for food. They pounded them into a kind of powdery flour and washed out the bitter taste with water."

"More clever Indians," said Laughing Water.

"Yes, more clever Indians," repeated Mrs. Grant. "The seed-gathering Indians lived in hot places where it was hard to grow vegetables; so they collected most of their food from wild plants: fruit and nuts and seeds.

"Did the seed-gathering Indians tell their little kids stories like you tell us stories all the time?" asked Singing Tree.

"Now, what is your idea in bringing that up?" asked Mrs. Grant. "Just what has storytelling to do with acorns?"

"Not anything, I suppose," said Singing Tree, "but I thought it would be nice for the little kids if the seed Indians would tell them stories."

"I have heard that old-fashioned Indians loved to tell their little children stories," said Mrs. Grant. "On long winter evenings they gathered around their fires to tell about wars and hunting and other adventures that had happened to their tribe years before. I'm sure all little Indian children knew a great many stories about their grandmas and grandpas; that is the way it ought to be for all little children. The Indians told other stories which we call legends; they were stories of make-believe in which the Indians tried to explain things which they really did not understand. Like they might have told a story that would somehow teach their children how the moon came to be in the sky or why woodpeckers drilled holes in trees. They did not really know the truth about such things, so they made up stories. Those legends were told by parents and grandparents, and when children grew up they passed them on to their children."

"You will have to start making legends for Laughing Water and me," said Singing Tree. "That way, we will know about everything, but exspecially why we eat candies."

"Oh, dear," said Mrs. Grant. "I don't know about you, Singing Tree. If you are throwing out a little hint to Mamma about giving you a candy, you might as well save your energy!"

Chapter 9

Fire! Fire!

"Mamma, come quick!" Singing Tree cried, bursting into the kitchen where Mrs. Grant had just finishing waxing the floor. "Come, quick!" she shrieked. "Hurry, Mamma!"

Mrs. Grant felt, no doubt, judging by the tone of Singing Tree's voice, that a real emergency had arisen.

"Meet Mamma at the front door!" she ordered, to get Singing Tree off the sticky kitchen floor. Then she raced around to the front door and down the steps. "Where? What is the matter?"

Singing Tree pointed down the drive.

"What is it? Take me to it!" ordered Mrs. Grant.

Halfway down the drive Mrs. Grant began to feel a little foolish chasing frantically after something, but not knowing what.

"Where are you taking me?" she asked, all out of breath and growing red in the face.

"Why, Mamma, can't you see what I can see?" asked Singing Tree, slowing to a halt. "Look at the cows! They're all lying in the grass getting a nice suntan. They'll look splendish when they are all suntanned."

"Oh, no!" moaned Mrs. Grant. "You mean to tell me you tracked up my kitchen floor and gave me that scare just to show me the cows lying in the sun?"

"Yes, Mamma," said Singing Tree. "It is very impertent for cows to get a suntan. That way they won't be able to crawl through fences and get in Mr. Blake's field, you see."

"Oh," Mrs. Grant moaned. "What can happen next?"

"I tell you what will happen next," said Singing Tree. "Lady is on the garden. That is what will happen next, Mamma."

"I'm afraid Lady is a very naughty dog," Mrs. Grant complained. "She knows as well as I do that she shouldn't be on the garden breaking the little plants."

"Lady! Come off that garden!" Mrs. Grant called in a sharp voice. "You know you shouldn't be on that garden, you naughty dog!"

Lady came out of the garden at once, her head down, her tail dragging between her legs.

"See," said Mrs. Grant, "she knew very well she should not be walking on the garden. See how ashamed she seems. Dogs act the way people act sometimes, you know."

"Yes, Mamma, they do," agreed Singing Tree, "betcept people don't put their ears down like Lady does."

Singing Tree had just had her hair shampooed, and Celia put the hair dryer on her head because the family was going to town and her hair needed to dry quickly. Richard said, "How do you like getting your hair dry that way, little Indian? Quite a fancy way to do it, isn't it?"

"Do you mind if I say something?" Singing Tree yelled above the noise of the dryer which sounded very loud in her ears but not so loud in Richard's ears.

"Of course not," smiled Richard. "Say all you want to say. Go ahead."

"Do you mind if I say something?" Singing Tree yelled again, not having heard Richard's remarks. "I'd like to say, Richard, that even though you're a big boy I can't possibly hear a word you're saying."

When Singing Tree had finished drying her hair, she heard Jamey call from his room, "Mother, I'd like to have a powwow with you before we leave for town. It's quite important."

Singing Tree's expression showed her wonder. "What's a pow-wow that Jamey wants?" she asked.

"You answer that one while I talk to Mother," Jamey said to Richard. "That will save Mother some time, and it will save Singing Tree from dying of curiosity."

"I don't want to die," said Singing Tree. "If I died Mamma would have only one little Indian, and she could not stand that.

She has to have two Indians or she will be incomptible. All I want is for you to tell me what is a powwow."

Richard grinned, as was his habit every time he looked at Singing Tree.

"Indians had powwows," Richard told her. "When the families of Indians had any problems, the old and important men got together and talked about the problems. They were very serious talks, and the Indians called them powwows."

"Did they talk a long time like the man in church when I am hungry and tired?" Singing Tree asked, a frown spreading over her face.

"Oh, sometimes they talked much longer than the man in church," Richard told her. "Sometimes they talked for hours."

"I'm glad I'm not a powwow Indian," said Singing Tree. "That way, I can get my dinner when I want it and I can go barefoot when I want to."

"What does barefoot have to do with a powwow?" asked Richard.

"You are a big boy," said Singing Tree, "and so you ought to know that barefoot is a special thing that's not meant for powwow Indians."

"Oh," Richard sighed. "There are still many things for me to learn, I fear."

In one of the large stores in town Mrs. Grant waited a long time to be served. Impatiently, Celia said, "It is always the same in this store; when you don't need help you have six people asking to serve you, and when you need help there is no one in sight."

"Send out some smoke signals," Jamey suggested. "That would get someone coming on the run."

Laughing Water turned troubled eyes on Jamey.

"You mean to burn the store down?" she asked.

"Not really," said Celia. "We'll tell you what that means on the way home. It would take too long now."

As soon as the groceries and new clothes were put in the trunk of the car, Singing Tree, with an elephant's memory for promises made to her, said, "Who is going to tell Laughing Water about smoke simples? She is in a hurry to hear about smoke simples."

73

"Er— I think the word is *signals*," Jamey corrected, clearing his throat. "Celia, seeing it is Laughing Water who wants to hear all about smoke signals, you'd better get her beside you and whisper in her ear."

"No! No!" cried Singing Tree. "I want to hear too. Smoke simples are inpertent things, and I want to know as much about them as Laughing Water does. Good Indians should share things, but exspecially smoke simples!"

"Er— The word is *signals*," Jamey repeated.

Celia said, "The long-ago Indians did not have telephones or radios or television to help them send messages to each other when they were long distances apart, and they didn't write letters to each other because they did not read or write until the white men taught them, so they got the clever idea of sending messages by using smoke signals. They would make a fire on a hill or big rock so that it could be seen a long way off. Before the fire grew too bright with flames, an Indian would put some green leaves or weeds on it to make a thick smoke which would float into the sky. By placing a heavy blanket over the smoldering fire, the Indian could hold back the smoke for a little time; then when he lifted the blanket, the smoke would rise in the kind of column he wished, according to the message he wanted to give. Each time the Indian lifted the blanket, out would puff a little cloud of smoke. Then he would cover the fire again. The Indians who were watching from far away would see the puffs of smoke and read the message they sent. They could answer with their own fire and blankets and puffs of smoke."

"Clever old-fashioned Indians!" said Laughing Water.

"But the smoke signals could not be seen at night," Jamey added, "so the Indians built big blazing fires to send messages after dark. When they built one fire the message said, 'All Indians who see this please pay attention.' Two fires said, 'All is well.' Three fires said, 'We need help,' and four fires said, 'Come to our camp.' "

"Four fires could have also said, 'Come to our powwow,' " added Celia. "I suppose the Indians grew very excited when they saw four fires burning side by side in the night."

Mrs. Grant should not have felt so surprised the next morning when, long before anyone was usually out of bed, she smelled smoke.

"Mr. Parsons is burning trash in his incinerator, before the wind starts to blow," she decided, and almost turned over for another hour's sleep.

She changed her mind when she heard someone cough. She slipped out of bed and sniffed at the air through the open window to find if the smoke smell was coming from out of doors. Her heart began to thump hard when she realized that the smoky smell came from inside the house.

She dragged on her robe and hurried from room to room sniffing as she moved. Laughing Water was fast asleep, curled up in a snug ball, but when Mrs. Grant looked at Singing Tree's bed, she found the covers thrown back and the bed empty. All the time, the smell of smoke came increasingly stronger to Mrs. Grant's nostrils. When she opened the door of the stairway leading to the basement, she had no doubt where the smoke was coming from. She raced, barefooted, down the fourteen steps. Before she reached the bottom she could see through the smoky haze what was going on. Singing Tree sat on the concrete floor, a towel in her hands, watching with a pleased and happy glow on her face as a fire of crumpled newspapers burned.

Mrs. Grant could see by the amount of ashes on the floor that a number of newspapers had already burned. Brown, burned spots scarred the once good green bath towel.

"Singing Tree, you naughty, naughty girl!" Mrs. Grant cried. "Whatever are you doing now?" She grabbed the towel and used it to smother the flames. Her question seemed unnecessary, even to her. She already knew what the whole scene meant—Indian smoke signals!

"I'm a simple Indian," sang Singing Tree, looking surprised that her mother was upset. "A smoke simple Indian," she added. "That's what I wanted to be most of all. That way, I can keep warm when it is cold. The fire will keep me warm."

"Where did you find matches?" asked Mrs. Grant, who always kept matches carefully hidden and had asked the rest of the family

75

Singing Tree knelt on the basement floor, happily fanning the smoking fire with a green bath towel.

to do the same since the small Indians had joined them.

"Old-fashioned Indians didn't have matches, Jamey told me, Mamma," said the little Indian. "He said they rubbed sticks together to make fires. He said it takes a long time to do that, and I didn't have a long time. I had to send my secret messages before everyone got up. I was lucky because I just got the last one sent when you came down the stairs."

"Where did you get the *matches?*" demanded Mrs. Grant, her voice becoming very firm.

"I didn't," said Singing Tree. "I did this." She screwed up a piece of newspaper until it formed a long taper; then she turned on one of the burners of the electric range which Mrs. Grant used in the basement when she had extra cooking to do. When the burner glowed red with heat, Singing Tree put the long taper of newspaper against it and it immediately burst into flames.

"Where did you learn to do that?" Mrs. Grant cried.

"Mr. Mahoney did it when he couldn't find the matches when he was in a hurry to light the fire on a cold morning," said Singing Tree. "Mr. Mahoney was clever, but he wasn't an old-fashioned Indian."

Mrs. Grant took the burning newspaper from Singing Tree and threw it into the big wood furnace which kept the house warm through the winter.

A few minutes later, while Mrs. Grant was still lecturing Singing Tree about the dangers of playing with fire and warning her that little girls could be burned to death if their clothing caught fire, Mr. Grant padded down the basement steps in his pajamas and slippers, sniffing sleepily at the smoke. He took one look at his wife with the little Indian and stopped short.

"Smoke signals, no doubt," he muttered and, with just a bewildered shake of his head, climbed back up the steps and returned to bed.

Chapter 10

Chicken-Fruit Pie

On a hot, sunny summer morning Mrs. Grant was putting the last roller in her hair when Singing Tree made her appearance to watch the operation.

"Ah, I smell something!" said Mrs. Grant, sniffing around Singing Tree's face. "I smell something, I'm sure! Now, whatever can it be? Oh, yes, I think I know; it's peanut butter! You have been eating peanut butter while Mamma was in the shower, haven't you?"

"Oops! Mamma, I should have had enough sense to wash myself so you couldn't smell me, shouldn't I?" Singing Tree said, not at all embarrassed.

"That wouldn't make it right to steal peanut butter while Mamma was in the shower," said Mrs. Grant. "It is wrong for little girls to steal food, but it is worse for them to steal and then try to hide the fact."

"It would be much betterest to just take the peanut butter without stealing it, wouldn't it, Mamma?"

"Oh, Singing Tree!" sighed Mrs. Grant. "Does anything I say to you ever sink in?"

"Of course it does, Mamma!" answered Singing Tree, rubbing her cheek against her mother's. "You teached me to wash dishes and they sink in the bubbly water, you know."

"Oh, me!" Mrs. Grant groaned, trying to hold back a grin.

"Do you feel all right, Mamma? Have you a pain somewhere? You sound kind of groany," said Singing Tree. "What can I do so you won't keep on being groany?"

"Now, let me see," Mrs. Grant said. "I think you can help Mamma most by trying hard to be a good girl today."

Singing Tree nodded in solemn agreement.

As Mrs. Grant was cleaning the bathroom later that morning she could hear that things weren't going very well with the children outdoors. She did not feel surprised a few minutes later to see Singing Tree in the bathroom doorway, tears dripping everywhere.

"Whatever is the matter this time?" asked Mrs. Grant.

"They're mean to me, Mamma!" cried Singing Tree. "Just horrible mean! Laughing Water is selfish. She won't let me play in her mud, and I want to play in her mud. She won't share like a Zuñi Indian. I know the Zuñi Indians shared their mud and didn't be selfish with it."

"So that's it," said Mrs. Grant. "And what about Jamey? Didn't I hear you yelling at Jamey?"

"Yes, I yelled at Jamey," howled Singing Tree. "I yelled because he wouldn't *die* for me. I was playing I was a bad Indian and he was a white man trying to live at my hunting ground, just like you said about the old-fashioned Indians; I shooted him with my pretent bow and arrow and he wouldn't *die* for me! Jamey says he's too young to die—even to pretend to die, and I want him to die, else he's spoiling all my fun."

"You don't really need Laughing Water's mud," said Mrs. Grant. "There is enough mud out there for a dozen Indians, and if Jamey doesn't want to die, why don't you play some other game? Now, I don't want any more crying and I don't want you to be acting like a little baby!"

A little while later when Mrs. Grant was cleaning the kitchen windows she heard Singing Tree yelling at Laughing Water again.

"Come indoors, Singing Tree, I want to talk to you," Mrs. Grant called.

She took Singing Tree on her lap. "I think you must be tired, or you're too hot, or you're sick," she said, cuddling Singing Tree and rocking her back and forth. "Little girls who cry so easily and act so miserable need to lie down and take a good rest. You take a nap in your bed, and when you feel better there will be some pastry for you and Laughing Water to make some little pies of your own. Mamma is going to make some gooseberry pies this morning, you know."

79

"What kind of pies, Mamma?"

"Gooseberry."

The pie making went on. Mrs. Grant noticed as she rolled out the pastry that no noise was coming from Singing Tree's room. "She really did fall asleep," Mrs. Grant told herself. "I knew she was tired. She'll be her happy little self again when she wakes up."

When she had put the four gooseberry pies in the oven, Mrs. Grant tiptoed to see if Singing Tree was still asleep. Singing Tree's bed was empty.

She looked out the window but could not see Singing Tree. Then she returned to the kitchen and asked through the open window, "Has anybody seen Singing Tree?"

"She went in to you," said Jamey. "We haven't seen her since then."

Mrs. Grant finally found Singing Tree in the basement. Singing Tree had found the shoe-polishing kit and had painted her forehead, cheeks, and chin a bright red with liquid shoe polish.

"Oh, Singing Tree, how *could* you? You were supposed to be asleep!"

"I got happy fast, Mamma," the little Indian said. "It was like you said. Just a *little* nap made me happy. My face is rosy now, I think, and that shows I am happy when I'm rosy."

"I guess it will just have to wear off," Mrs. Grant said later to her husband. "I've tried soap and water and cold cream, but I'm afraid to rub too hard for fear of hurting her skin. Right now she looks as though she is wearing war paint."

"What's war paint?" asked Singing Tree. "I didn't crystalize that you could paint wars."

Jamey cleared his throat. "The word is *realize*," he said, "and no one is talking about painting wars. The old-fashioned Indians often painted themselves when they went to war. That is what Mamma is talking about."

In the evening Mrs. Grant and the two little Indians were at home alone when the thunderstorm rolled in on their hot, uncomfortable world. The wind raged and howled, lightning flashed across the sky, and the thunder grumbled and mumbled, in the distance at first; but when it came closer, it boomed and roared right overhead. Darkness fell quickly with heavy, black clouds scudding across the sky. After one big flash of lightning and a monstrous clap of thunder, the house suddenly plunged into darkness. The girls cried in terror and clung to their mother.

"Come, now, let us not be afraid," Mrs. Grant said. "It's just that the electric power has gone off. We'll say the little prayer I taught you."

The sobbing quieted, but not enough to enable the two girls to pray, so Mrs. Grant took them on her lap and said the prayer for them:

"Jesus, tender Shepherd, hear me;
Bless Thy little lamb tonight;
Through the darkness be Thou near me;
Keep me safe till morning light."

The weeping stopped, and the children helped Mrs. Grant grope past the furniture toward the big living-room window. Looking across the river to the highway and freeway, they could see the lights of cars and trucks hurrying on their way; but not a light shone from the windows of houses.

"This is what you'd call a real blackout," said Mrs. Grant. "That is, until the lightning flashes again."

They watched and waited a long time before they saw the family car moving slowly along the river road. Mrs. Grant hunted in the darkness and found some candles. She had them lighted and the table set for the evening meal when Mr. Grant and the children came indoors.

"Guess what, Daddy!" cried Singing Tree. "We had a great big blew out! It's lots of fun having a big blew out! We get to light the candles!"

"In fact, it has been so much fun," Mrs. Grant said with a smile, "that Singing Tree and Laughing Water had a big crying match about it. They sounded ridiculously happy, I can assure you!"

"Do you think the old-fashioned Indians would be scared if they were in a storm, Mamma?" asked Laughing Water.

"That is really hard for me to say," Mrs. Grant replied. "They

81

had a legend about thunder and lightning. It said that a great bird flew in the sky when the thunder was heard; the rumbling was the sound of the thunderbird flapping its wings, they claimed. The Indians thought that if one of them was hit by lightning and lived he was some magic kind of person."

"Guess what Mamma made for supper!" Laughing Water said. "Mamma made chicken-fruit pie! Yummy!"

"Chicken-fruit pie!" repeated Celia. "I haven't ever heard of chicken fruit. Where does it grow?"

"Would you guess, gooseberry pie?" asked Jamey, trying to sound serious.

"Oh, you girls!" giggled Celia. "What will these little Indians come up with next?"

Chapter 11

That Stupid Rule!

Without much warning for the little Indians the Grants added three more girls to their family. Singing Tree and Laughing Water felt delighted at first when Mrs. Grant told them that three more sisters were coming to join the family.

"We won't have to ask other kids to come and play with us now," Singing Tree said, jigging around the kitchen in excitement; but Singing Tree's usually happy feet were dragging after the new children had been with them only one day. Liza, Peggy, and Bonnie had not lived in a home where the children were loved and well-cared for; they had no idea that a home was meant to be peaceful and happy. Nor did they understand how to share or to love each other. Quarrels and fistfights broke out among them every few minutes. Every happening seemed an excuse for fighting. They bit and scratched, pulled hair, and pounded each other. Had they kept their quarrels among themselves, it might not have been so bad; but Singing Tree and Laughing Water, who scarcely knew what it meant to fight, became targets of their cruelty. They battered the little girls not only with their fists and fingernails but with cruel words too.

One morning Mrs. Grant was stirring a pot of relish over the stove when enraged cries coming from the back lawn caused her to drop her spoon. The spoon clattered to the floor, splattering red and green relish, but Mrs. Grant hardly noticed.

"You yellow skin! You dirty Indian! I hate you, Laughing Water!"

Mrs. Grant recognized Liza's shrill voice. "This is really terrible!" she gasped. "Much worse than having to grab my walking shoes every hour or so to run off looking for Singing Tree."

She straightened her red-and-white apron and tried to calm the rapid beating of her heart before opening the kitchen door. Five very unhappy faces turned to her as she settled herself on the back-porch steps.

"Liza," she said, trying to keep her voice steady, "did you know that Laughing Water took a bath last night and washed herself this morning?"

Liza scowled. "Yes, I suppose I know that."

"Then what makes you think she is a *dirty Indian?*"

"Everyone knows Indians are dirty things!" Liza snapped. "Everyone who knows anything knows that anyone who isn't white is a dirty, filthy creature!" Liza cried, her voice growing louder.

"Oh, I didn't know that," said Mrs. Grant, still trying to keep her voice normal, but hearing it rise despite herself. "Do you recall that when the welfare lady brought you at the beginning of this week you and your sisters were *quite* dirty? That made no difference to our family, wanting to give you a home and take care of you. Singing Tree and Laughing Water do not look like you looked standing there at the front door when I first saw you."

"We weren't dirty!" snapped Liza. "Not the kind of dirty I mean about Indians, anyway. That's dirty in a different way."

Mrs. Grant persisted. "You were dirty, your clothes were ragged and filthy, and you had no shoes to wear," she reminded them. "I think you will remember the hours Celia and I spent in bathing you, washing your hair and curling it, and buying all those nice new clothes for you. All that we did was make you clean and pretty on the outside. Laughing Water and Singing Tree are also clean and pretty on the outside; the only difference between you and them now is the color of your skins. That really isn't the important thing, you know. The outside means nothing, really. It is what a person is inside himself that matters—whether he is kind and good and honest and loving—that is what counts. The skin color tells us nothing of what a person really is; you understand?"

Liza glowered at Mrs. Grant.

"While you live with us," Mrs. Grant went on, "there is one thing I will not tolerate, and that is your calling either of the girls *dirty Indian* again. There is too much hate in this world already; we cannot have it here in our home. No, certainly not!"

She turned to go indoors. "As soon as the relish is in the jars, we'll all work together in the garden," she told the scowling girls. "There is plenty of weeding to be done, and I think a little work might ease the fighting around here."

"Irk!" shuddered Peggy, the second-oldest girl. "Who ever heard of weeding as a girl's job? I've never weeded in all my life!"

"I've heard of weeding in all my life, haven't I, Mamma?" asked Singing Tree. "Mamma says that those that don't work don't eat, so we'd better go to the garden and weed if we want to eat. 'Those that don't work don't eat' is Mamma's rule around here, isn't it, Mamma?"

Mrs. Grant gave each of the five girls a plot of garden to weed and showed them how to do it; then she went back to the house to prepare lunch.

"That rule that Mamma made is really stupid!" Peggy cried as soon as Mrs. Grant had closed the kitchen door behind her.

"Mamma didn't make that rule," Laughing Water said.

"Then who *did*?" Peggy asked, anger bristling in her voice. "I never worked at home, but I ate, so that rule wasn't at our house. It's a stupid rule!"

"I know what it really means," said Laughing Water, "and it really isn't stupid at all. Mamma says it is just a rule of life. You come over to the tomato patch and I'll show you what Mamma means about a rule of life."

Mrs. Grant watched through the open window as five girls stood around a tomato plant. Laughing Water leaned down and gently lifted a branch loaded with large green tomatoes. Under the branch every girl could see a tomato that was almost ripe.

"See that!" said Laughing Water proudly. "Singing Tree and I helped Mamma and Daddy plant the little tomato plants, and then we helped take care of them by weeding and watering and sometimes hoeing. In a few more days some more tomatoes will be turning pink. Soon we'll be able to have them in a nice salad."

"Yummy!" said Peggy and Liza, looking pleasant for the first time since they had come into the garden. Bonnie, the little one,

85

clapped her hands and squealed, "Goody! Goody!"

"We hardly ever had tomatoes at home," Peggy said. "That was because no one made a garden, and we didn't have enough money to buy them at the store."

"See what I *mean!*" cried Laughing Water. "You didn't have tomatoes because you didn't make a garden and work to make things grow. Because you didn't work, you didn't eat!"

Peggy stared at Laughing Water in an unbelieving way and then shrugged her shoulders. "Oh, I still don't care! It's a stupid rule, anyway!"

More grumbling and quarreling than weeding went on in the garden that morning. But Singing Tree and Laughing Water had finished their plots when Mrs. Grant called that lunch was ready and those who had finished their jobs could come to eat.

Liza called after them as they walked towards the house, "Goody, goody Indians with dirty skins and white hearts!"

"Now, don't let's have any weeping!" Mrs. Grant said when she saw that the little Indians' mouths trembled. "The girls haven't been taught to be kind and loving to each other or to anyone else, and we must feel sorry for them. I think it would be good for all of us if we'd just sit around and smoke the peace pipe together."

That made the little Indians stop crying in an instant.

"You said it wasn't good for people to smoke, Mamma!" exclaimed Singing Tree, looking as puzzled as her sister.

Mrs. Grant smiled. "I know I did, honey," she said, "and I meant it. What Mamma meant by smoking the peace pipe was that we should learn to show friendliness and get along nicely together, learn to understand each other and not to be always angry and ill-tempered. The old-fashioned Indians smoked their peace pipes as a sign that all who were smoking together wanted to be friendly and kind to each other. People today often say 'Let us smoke the peace pipe,' meaning, 'Let's stop quarreling and have everything peaceful between us.' "

"I want something to eat, Mamma," Singing Tree said, rubbing the front of her dress. "I'm a starved little Indian. That's what I am. I worked and now I eat. That's the rule of life, you know, Mamma."

Mrs. Grant turned to the stove, biting her lip to hold back her laughter. "Those who don't wash hands don't eat," she said, trying to keep the chuckle out of her voice as she dipped big bowls of steaming vegetable soup.

Hard days followed for the little Indians. Liza, Peggy, and Bonnie broke their toys and tore their books. They stole the pennies the Indians had saved, and they stole some of Laughing Water's and Singing Tree's clothes and hid them in their own drawers, even though they had been outfitted with lovely new clothes of their own. Two reasonably happy little Indians now became dull, sad little Indians.

Then one day the welfare lady came to take the girls back to their own home. When they had left, Laughing Water said, "Mamma, why were the girls like that? Why were they so mean?"

"The poor little things had such *ugly* lives," Mrs. Grant said. "Terrible things have happened to them which have made them mean and unloving. Perhaps if they could be kept in a kind, loving home for a long time they would change."

That night Laughing Water and Singing Tree lay quietly in their beds, their eyes wide open and their ears straining for household sounds long after they should have been asleep. They could hear a buzzing conversation, and they knew that Mrs. Grant and Celia were in the kitchen talking as they often did. Occasionally their alert little Indian ears would pick up a few sentences, which they filed neatly in the storerooms of their minds to be talked over and used by them later as they played house together. Playing "Mamma and Celia" had become a favorite pastime.

They could recognize the sound of Mrs. Grant speaking, but she spoke too quietly for them to understand. But when Celia spoke, her voice came to them more clearly.

"I believe you're right," Celia said. "The time was not ripe. It's all very sad. Those three girls needed time to forget their terrible homelife, but we could not just sit and wait while they abused our little Indians. The time just was not ripe," she repeated.

The next morning when Mrs. Grant was zipping up the back

of Singing Tree's sun dress, the child said, "Mamma, when does time get ripe?"

"You mean the thyme in the garden? The little herb plants near the rhubarb?" asked Mrs. Grant.

"I don't know," Singing Tree answered. "Celia said it to you; she told you that the time was not ripe. But she didn't say a thing about the rebarb."

Mrs. Grant felt very puzzled indeed. She tried to think of what she and Celia had done in the garden the day before. She chased through her mind for what she might have said about the time but could find nothing.

"When did Celia say those things to me?" she asked.

Singing Tree suddenly became very interested in the pattern on the rug beside her bed.

"Ooooh!" Mrs. Grant cooed, light breaking through the mists of her mind. "I see, now! Who was listening again when it was time for all good Indians to be fast asleep? I think Celia and I had better have our little talks in the basement from now on."

"You don't need to do that, Mamma," said Singing Tree. "You'd get tippifically tired coming all the way up the basement stairs to bed, you know."

"I think the word is *terrifically,*" Mrs. Grant reminded her. "And, you know something? I think the exercise on the basement stairs would be good for me.

"Now let's get back to the first question about the time being ripe; Celia did not mean the herbs in the garden at all. We were talking about Liza and Peggy and Bonnie. They were naughty girls and at times very hateful because they had never been taught to love. Mamma said they need a new birth, which simply means that they needed to let Jesus clean all the ugliness, meanness, and hate out of their hearts and fill them with love. He can make our hearts and minds brand-new.

"It would take time to help the girls to understand all that, you see. Celia said the time was not ripe, meaning that there was not enough time to teach the girls before they were taken away."

Mrs. Grant shook her head sadly. "Oh, but I had hoped when they learned to sing 'I'm a Child of the King' and 'Jesus Loves

*As Mrs. Grant helped the girls to get dressed, they asked
about what they had overheard the night before.*

Me' with you, that the words would begin to work on their minds. I hope they'll remember the times Mamma prayed with them and talked with them; perhaps, too, they will think of the things the teachers told them at church. Maybe someday these memories will make a difference in their lives."

"Does Jesus need to clean out Singing Tree's heart and my heart?" asked Laughing Water.

"Oh, yes," replied Mrs. Grant. "There isn't anyone in the world who does not need a clean heart so that Jesus' love can live there. Not a single person in all the world."

"I don't want to be ugly," said Singing Tree. "I want Jesus to fix up my heart, brand-new. You getted the time ripe for me, Mamma. We've been at our new house long enough to know that Jesus loves us."

Mrs. Grant said, "Jesus would be very happy if you both asked Him to make your hearts clean so that His love can live in there. Would you like me to say prayers with you and ask Jesus to do that?"

"Oh, yes!" said Singing Tree, sliding to her knees.

"Me, too, Mamma," Laughing Water nodded, and knelt beside her sister and mother. Mrs. Grant put her arms around the little Indians and told Jesus the girls wanted to give their hearts to Him and that they wanted to be loving and kind all their lives. When they rose from their knees Mrs. Grant said, "I want you both to think a lot about this; I want you to remember all your lives that Jesus loves you very much and that He wants His love to be in your hearts forever."

Chapter 12

The Stingingest Day

The day had dawned hot and steamy, and by noon the temperature was still climbing higher and higher.

"I'm hot!" Singing Tree complained after eating only a few bites from her sandwich. "May we play in the shade under the big oak tree, Mamma? And may we run under the sprinklers in the pasture whenever we feel too hot?"

"That's a splendid idea!" Mrs. Grant exclaimed. "That will give me a little peace and quiet while you are out of the house."

Those turned out to be some more of Mrs. Grant's famous last words. The peace and quiet lasted only a few minutes before she heard Singing Tree crying away down the drive.

"Oh, dear! What can it be now?" she wondered. "I hope it's nothing too serious."

The tone and volume of Singing Tree's howling soon made Mrs. Grant believe that, whatever had happened, it must have been more serious than most of the things that could cause Singing Tree to cry. She raced to the living room and looked out the window. Laughing Water was carrying her sister up the drive. She was staggering, almost falling several times; for Singing Tree weighed almost as much as she, although Laughing Water was two years older.

When they got close enough to the house for Mrs. Grant's voice to be heard above Singing Tree's howls, she called, "Put her down, Laughing Water! You'll ruin your back!"

Laughing Water stood her sister on the ground then, and the younger one continued bellowing like a young bull; she limped so badly Mrs. Grant was sure her foot must be cut almost in two.

Mrs. Grant ran to meet them. "Whatever is the *matter?*" She

91

had expected to see blood oozing from the foot, but she couldn't see a drop.

"A big bee stung her," Laughing Water said.

Mrs. Grant almost collapsed from relief mixed with rising annoyance. "It stung her on the foot, I suppose?" Mrs. Grant said.

"Oh, no; whatever gave you that idea, Mamma?" asked Laughing Water. "She was stung in the corner of the eye. Can't you see it swelling already?"

"And she's limping?" Mrs. Grant asked. "How could a sting in the corner of the eye make her *limp*?"

Laughing Water just shook her head while Singing Tree went right on bellowing. When Mrs. Grant tried to remove the sting from her flesh, she bellowed twice as loud as before.

"Now, look here!" Mrs. Grant said, trying to drown out Singing Tree. "I really don't think a bee sting hurts quite as bad as that! Come over to the garden faucet with me, and I'll put some old-fashioned Indian medicine on the sting. In no time you won't even know anything happened to you!"

The children looked really surprised when their mother took a daub of mud from the wet earth under the faucet and painted the skin around Singing Tree's eye with it. Almost at once the bellowing stopped.

"It doesn't hurt now," said Singing Tree, brightening. "That was magic mud, Mamma."

"I used to put mud on Jamey's and Richard's and Celia's stings," Mrs. Grant said. "I was told that is what the old-fashioned Indians did for their stings, and it really works."

Later in the day, Laughing Water noticed that a wasp was going in and out of a small hole in the stone wall along the front of the house.

"Let's have some fun," she told Singing Tree. "I think the wasp is going in there with its loads of mud to build a house. I'll block the hole, and won't the wasp be surprised when he comes back with another load of mud and can't find his hole!"

Laughing Water found a stone from the drive which was just the right size and shape. She stuck it firmly into the hole in the wall. Soon the wasp flew back with another load of mud. The girls giggled as it hummed and buzzed and zoomed around searching for its hole.

"You were right, Laughing Water. He looks like a very surprised wasp," Singing Tree said.

It landed, at last, on the stone Laughing Water had used to block its entrance hole. Then up into the air it zoomed and circled Laughing Water several times. Before she could realize what was about to happen, the wasp made a sharp dive at her, stung her on the chin, and disappeared in a wink.

Now Laughing Water bellowed!

Mrs. Grant came running. "What now?" she asked, thinking of that peace and quietness she was supposed to be enjoying.

"I'm stung!" yelled Laughing Water, holding her chin.

"All right! All right!" said Mrs. Grant. "Let's get that magic Indian medicine working again."

With a little cake of mud oozing on her chin, Laughing Water was able to find a smile again.

"I can't understand why you girls are being stung," said Mrs. Grant. "Were you teasing the wasp, Laughing Water?"

Laughing Water's head drooped a little. "I plugged the hole in the rock wall where the wasp was going through with its load of mud," she said. "I think it must have smelled me on the rock, and it stung me because I was mean to it."

"That's interesting," said Mrs. Grant, her eyebrows raised, "and may I ask what was going on when Singing Tree was stung?"

"The big girl from the neighbors' house said she betted we couldn't hit the bee nest in the big oak tree," said Singing Tree. "She threw some rocks at the nest and said, 'See how mad the bees can get? I'll bet you can't hit them the way I do!'

"So Laughing Water threw some rocks. She hit the bee house better'n the other girl, and then the other girl said, 'What's the matter with you, Singing Tree? Can't *you* throw rocks and hit the bees?'

"I showed that big girl I can hit the bee house betterest of all us kids. Did the bees get mad! They rushed everywhere and bumped each other. One bee bumped into me, and I hit at it

93

because I hate bees bizzying in my hair. It got madder then and stung me."

"Oh, I *see!*" said Mrs. Grant. "I suppose the moral to both those stories is not to tease wasps and bees."

"What's a moral?" asked Singing Tree.

"It's a kind of lesson taught you by something that happens to you," Mrs. Grant told her.

"Oh," said Singing Tree brightly, "I'll get morals at school every day, won't I? Betcept recesses, of course. Recesses won't be morals."

"Oh, dear!" smiled Mrs. Grant. "Walking shoes or no walking shoes, how can I ever expect to win?"

"You can't win with walking shoes, Mamma," said Singing Tree. "What you need to win a race is Jamey's track shoes with spikes in them. He told me that, so it's right, Mamma."

In the evening, when Mrs. Grant was getting ready to take her shower, her family heard her yell.

"Whatever's happened?" they all wondered. Mrs. Grant did not often yell.

She came from the bathroom, limping.

"I need a nice daub of good, old-fashioned Indian mud," she said with a sheepish smile.

"You been teaching bees, Mamma?" asked Singing Tree.

"You been teasing wasps, Mamma?" asked Laughing Water.

"Nothing quite like that," answered Mrs. Grant. "I stepped into the shower without switching on the light and trod on a big, fat bumblebee. Don't ask me what she was doing in the shower room!"

"Aren't you glad you have Indians, Mamma?" Singing Tree asked as Jamey came in with a generous daub of magic mud. Betcept you wouldn't know how to stop things stinging if you didn't have Indians."

"This has been the stingingest day you ever heard of," Jamey said. "I think I'll buzz off to bed before I am attacked!"

"I just thought of an old Indian saying," announced Mrs. Grant. "It goes something like this: 'A wise man does not put his eye to a wasp's nest to see if it is at home.'"

94

"There's another one I recall," Celia said with a smile. "It says: 'All creatures are kind if you are polite to them.' Everyone take note: Don't block up wasps' nests. Don't tease bees, and *don't* tread on bumblebees!"

After that long, hot, stingingest day, the Indians finally got to bed and, looking in on them, Mrs. Grant limped back to the living room and said, "They seem to be asleep now. I hope to-morrow goes better for them."

After a while Mr. Grant looked up from his reading and said, "You know, I believe Singing Tree is improving at last. She hasn't been into half as many things lately, has she? Don't you think she is doing better?"

Without answering, Mrs. Grant sat up very straight and said, "What do I smell?"

She sniffed several times, then Mr. Grant began to sniff, too. "It smells like insect spray," he said.

As Mrs. Grant neared the girls' room, the air was thick with insect spray; she could hardly breathe. Light came from their room. When Mrs. Grant looked in, she found Singing Tree standing in the middle of the room squirting spray in all directions. She and Laughing Water were both giving choking coughs.

"Stop!" Mrs. Grant cried. "Whatever do you think you are doing?"

"I don't think I am doing anything," said the little Indian. "I'm just getting rid of those bizzy, bizzy little meskitnoes. We've had enough stings today! I cerpently don't want any more."

"Why did you spray so much?" Mrs. Grant gasped. "Just one or two quick squirts would have been plenty. Both of you go to the back porch and breathe some fresh air."

"I was just doing what it said," said Singing Tree. "You read to me on the can that it *lasts for hours*. It said it lasts for hours so I sprayed for hours, just like it said."

Mrs. Grant's hands went to her forehead. "Oh, no!" she said.

To Mr. Grant, who now stood in the bedroom doorway, gasping a little, she said, "What was that you were saying about someone's not getting into things?"

The summer days were passing quickly.

"I haven't heard the kingbirds lately," Jamey remarked to his mother one morning. "The babies must be 'launched' and on their own, now."

"That's probably true," replied Mrs. Grant. "They will have to fly south for the winter, so they need practice in caring for themselves before they start such a hazardous trip."

"Will they come back here next spring?" asked Laughing Water.

"I hope they do," Mrs. Grant said. "I'm sure we would all miss them if they decided not to come back here after all the springs they have spent with us."

"I'll need lots of help today," Mrs. Grant announced. "I want to clean the house from one end to the other before school starts. Will two little Indians help me?"

"If the old-fashioned Indians helped white people, then these two Indians will help this white woman," said Laughing Water. "How much did Indians help the settlers, Mamma?"

"The way they helped most was to show the people how to live where they settled," Mrs. Grant answered. "They taught them how to put the things provided by this strange, new land to the best use. The Indians introduced new foods to the settlers, showing them how to get the food and how to cook it; in the snow country they showed them how to make sleds and snowshoes and goggles and moccasins. Sometimes they helped sick settlers with the special medicines they made from plants."

"Did the settlers do anything for the Indians when they were helped like that?" asked Laughing Water.

"Oh, yes," Mrs. Grant said. "The settlers had much better tools, which they shared with the Indians. They taught the Indians to read and write; they showed them how to make paper. We could possibly think of many more ways in which the two peoples helped each other."

"Are there many Indians now?" Laughing Water asked.

"Not nearly as many as there used to be," Mrs. Grant told her,

96

"but there are still a good many of them. Some of them still cling to the old-fashioned ways, but most of them live just as the rest of us live."

Celia and Jamey seemed to be playing a grand game in the living room. "Massachusetts!" cried Jamey.

"Omaha!" shouted Celia.

"Seattle!" said Jamey.

"Oklahoma!" replied Celia.

"Mississippi!"

"Michigan!— Oh, Jamey, I'm all out of breath!"

"What are they doing?" Laughing Water asked.

"I have a feeling they heard us talking about how the Indians and white people helped each other, so now they are trying to see which of them knows the greatest number of places with Indian names in the United States," Mrs. Grant said. "They have named just a very few, for we have Indian names in many, many places; they could probably go on as they have been for hours. Thinking of all those names reminds me that there is another way we received help from the Indians. That was that many of our roads and railroads today follow the old Indian trails which were made when they took trading journeys and moved from one camp to another."

"They were clever Indians to find their way through woods and mountains where no one had traveled before, weren't they, Mamma?" asked Laughing Water.

"Yes," said Mrs. Grant thoughtfully, "that's just another way the old-fashioned Indians were clever. Little Indians like you and Singing Tree need never feel ashamed that you are Indians. The people in your family way, way back were very clever, much cleverer than many people today with so many more chances to do well."

Mrs. Grant and Celia, with the girls' help, finished the house-cleaning just before school was to start. Brand-new school clothes, tennis shoes, and red rubber boots for winter waited in the closets. Paper, pencils, erasers, pens, crayons, all were ready, waiting for school to start.

97

Mr. Grant was ready to start another year of teaching the girls and boys of the village. Celia and Richard were waiting for college to begin, and Jamey felt anxious to return to high school.

Laughing Water felt glad to be going back to school to see again the friends she had made in the spring.

But the most excited one of all was Singing Tree. She waited, too, worried and anxious at one moment, eager and very chattery the next. What would first grade be like?

"Will the bus driver forget me the first afternoon?" she asked her mother for the fiftieth time.

"Now, look here!" Mrs. Grant said, "everything will be all right. Your teacher will put a little tag on your dress with Mr. Sam's name on it, so Mr. Sam will know you are to go home on his bus. Laughing Water will be there, and she, too, can make sure you get on the right bus. Anyway, what's all the fuss about? Mr. Sam knows you very well by now, and you know Mr. Sam. There isn't a thing in the world to worry about."

Chapter 13

Lost: Red Boots and Glasses

"This is wonderful!" Mrs. Grant exclaimed when another thunderstorm swept in and dumped buckets of rain on the thirsty, dusty earth. "It is just what we needed."

As suddenly as it had rushed in, the storm blew away, leaving the earth smelling sweet and clean. For Laughing Water and Singing Tree it left a good supply of ingredients for mud pies.

"Jamey, I need some carrots and onions from the garden to put in a stew for supper," Mrs. Grant said. "You and the girls put on your rubber boots and dig the vegetables for me, please."

Several minutes later Mrs. Grant heard Singing Tree weeping.

"Oh, dear! What now?" she asked herself as she headed for the basement stairs. "Singing Tree, what is the matter now?"

Tears ran down the little girl's chubby cheeks, which had grown rosy through the summer. No one, simply no one, could gush tears like Singing Tree. Mr. Grant claimed that she had the best supply of tears in seven counties.

Loud sobs were the only answer to Mrs. Grant's question.

"What's the matter with Mamma's Indian?" she asked. "Just whatever can it be this time?" Mrs. Grant stood there holding her hands together so that little plops of bread dough would not fall from them to the floor.

Finally Singing Tree was able to say, "Someone stole— Someone stole my—" but that was as far as she could get. She sounded like a cracked phonograph record.

"Wait until I wash the dough off my hands," said Mrs. Grant, "and then I'll hear all about it."

Soon she had Singing Tree on her lap. "Now, take a big, deep breath, pull yourself together, and stop crying," she said. "I

99

can't understand what you're saying when you cry at the same time; and if I don't understand what the matter is, how can I help you?"

After several minutes Singing Tree was sighing instead of sobbing as she leaned her head on Mrs. Grant's shoulder.

"There was a burglary, Mamma," she gasped in a whispering voice.

"A *what?*" asked Mrs. Grant, who should have been used to big words by now but wasn't.

"A burglary, I said. They stoled my red rubber boots you got me for going to school on rainy days."

"Oh," said Mrs. Grant. "A burglary! I see. Who do you mean by they?"

"The ones that stoled my slick red boots," Singing Tree said, getting herself pulled together. "I left those good red rubber boots in the bottom of my closet, just like you said, and now they are gone. They stoled them in the night."

"Are you sure they're gone?" Mrs. Grant asked.

"I'm perceptionally sure," Singing Tree answerd. "I put them there, and they're not there; so they must be gone."

"Sounds reasonable," said Mrs. Grant, "but let us look again just to make sure."

Hand in hand they went to the bedroom to look in the closet. It was quite true; the red boots had vanished.

"That's quite mysterious," said Mrs. Grant. "I'm sure no one stole them. I think you must have worn them yourself, Singing Tree. You probably left them somewhere. Remember that Mamma told you if you always put your shoes and boots in the closet as soon as you took them off, then they would never be lost?"

"But I did as you told me, Mamma!" mourned Singing Tree, all prepared to make another shower of tears. "I was the per-fectshedest Indian anyone could every unagerate."

"Oh, dear! That vocabulary of yours! It never ceases to amaze me!" Mrs. Grant said.

"What is that thing, Mamma? A vocavalrary? Is it on my face?"

100

"Vocabulary refers to the words you say. Oh, dear! I forgot my bread! You go and take another look for your boots while Mamma finishes putting the bread in the pans to rise again. I think you were the one who lost them, and you should make a good effort to find them."

As Mrs. Grant placed the last pan of bread in a warm place to rise before being put in the oven, she heard loud sobs coming from the children's room. Indeed, they were louder sobs than she had ever heard before.

Racing to the bedroom she found Singing Tree curled up on her bed, a ball of complete misery.

"What is it *now?*" she asked, sounding a little concerned, but also slightly weary of having one crisis after another.

"They *did* take my boots, Mamma," Singing Tree sobbed. "No one can purchwade me different. I looked everywhere, and my red boots are just inderwishable; that's the truth!"

Mrs. Grant sat on Singing Tree's bed. "I'd like to see you stop that dreadful crying," she said. "There really isn't anything to cry about. Your red boots can't be far away. They just couldn't walk out of the house overnight."

Singing Tree sprang to sitting position. "That's it, Mamma!" she said, suddenly very bright for a girl who, a few seconds before, had been utterly forlorn. "Boots are specialty for walking. They got tired of being locked in the closet, and they walked out in the night. They sneaked. Things that have feet can sneak in the night!"

"Oh, really!" said Mrs. Grant. "I have an idea. I think we ought to ask Jesus to help us find those red boots. I don't believe they walked, and Mamma doesn't have money to buy you another pair. You will need them when the heavy rains come and when there is snow on the ground. It is a rule at school, you know, that any child who has no waterproof boots cannot go beyond the breezeways to play during recesses. The teachers can't have little children tramping around in the snow and then coming to sit in school with sopping-wet shoes and socks. It would not be good for the children to sit with wet, cold feet, and it would make the classrooms messy. Come, kneel down with Mamma and let's talk

101

to Jesus about the red boots. You tell Jesus about your losing the boots, and I know He'll help us find them."

"But, Mamma, I wasn't the one that losted them, so I can't tell Jesus a lie. You tolded me Jesus knows when things are true and when they are a lie."

"All right, you tell Jesus what happened," Mrs. Grant agreed.

"Dear Jesus," Singing Tree prayed between loud sniffs, "my red boots sneaked out last night. Please tell the red boots to sneak back because Mamma doesn't have any more money left."

Mrs. Grant went to get her walking shoes. "We'll go and take a good look around the house," she said. "I know we'll find them."

As she and Singing Tree were leaving the house by way of the basement door, Mrs. Grant noticed an empty gunny sack which had held calves' mash lying on the basement floor. She picked it up and stared at what she saw under it. Little rubber boots that had at one time been shiny and bright red were now smothered with brown mud—blobs of thick mud that would not come off easily.

"Now, how did those boots get under that sack?" asked Mrs. Grant, "and *how* did they get so dirty? I can't understand how they could get in such a state!"

"I s'pose Jesus made them sneak under the big sack," said Singing Tree. "I s'pose He was deshamed to let them just sneak back to the closet so dirty."

"It was kind of Jesus to lead Mamma to lift up the sack and find the boots so I wouldn't have to waste a lot of time looking for them," Mrs. Grant said. "Thank You, Jesus," she said.

"Yes, Singing Tree says Thank You, Jesus, too," said Singing Tree.

Mrs. Grant sat on the basement couch and motioned to Singing Tree to join her. "I think you could tell me how those boots got under that sack and why they are so filthy," she said in a stern voice.

Singing Tree sat and stared at the red boots. Then she said, "I redember now; I took the red boots out to jump in the mud pie Laughing Water and I made behind the barn. You were taking a nap so you couldn't tell me not to take them out. It was too bad

102

you couldn't tell me that, wasn't it, Mamma?"

"Yes, it surely was," Mrs. Grant answered, "because now it will be very hard work for you to get them clean again; very hard work!"

Singing Tree tried to wipe away a huge tear that trickled down her cheek. "You aren't going to help me, Mamma?"

Mrs. Grant shook her head, meaning No! She showed Singing Tree how to scrape the lumpiest mud off the boots and then how to hose them but, although Singing Tree used a load of energy, she could not make them look again as they had when they were brand-new.

That evening at suppertime Mrs. Grant noticed that Singing Tree was not wearing the new glasses which the eye doctor said she must wear. She had been wearing glasses for several months. Mrs. Grant looked on the end of the kitchen counter, the special place Singing Tree had been given to put her glasses when she was not wearing them. They were not there. When Mrs. Grant asked about the glasses, Singing Tree glanced at Laughing Water in wide-eyed fashion.

"Come, now," Mr. Grant said. "What are you two hiding from us?"

"I put the glasses off to jump in the hay." Singing Tree spoke in a weak, squeaky voice. "You said to put them off if I had rough play to do." Staring at the white mound of mashed potato on her plate, she went on, "I put them on the big board, but when I finished playing they were not there. I think Henny Penny or Rooster Pooster must have wanted glasses so they could see worms better. That way they could get full and fat."

"Oh, no!" Mrs. Grant murmured, looking at her husband as though she would burst into tears at any moment. "I suppose she means she put them on the beam across the top of the barn. She could easily reach it from the highest bales of hay. How does one go about finding a small child's glasses in a barn filled with thirty tons of hay? How?

"That's forty-five dollars worth of glasses, you know," said Mr. Grant. "Looking for the needle in the haystack couldn't be any harder. I'm afraid that's about good-bye to those glasses!"

At bedtime Mrs. Grant said to Singing Tree, "We must talk

*Singing Tree hosed the mud from her boots, but she
could not make them as shiny as when they were new.*

to Jesus about those glasses. Forty-five dollars is a lot of money to find for another pair."

"Jesus helped us find the red boots," said Singing Tree, "so He'll help us find the glasses. It will be easy for Jesus to find the glasses if He can find red boots, because glasses are for seeing."

Mrs. Grant said, "You kneel here with me, Singing Tree, and I will talk to Jesus about the glasses." When the girls were ready she said, "Dear Father in heaven, you know what has happened to Singing Tree's glasses today. We are sorry that she was disobedient and did not put them in the right place when she took them off. Please help her by living in her heart as she wants You to, so that she will be obedient to her mamma and daddy. You know that we don't have forty-five dollars right now to get her new glasses, so please help us with our problem."

The next morning, as soon as it was light, Mrs. Grant, Jamey, Singing Tree, and Laughing Water searched the barn for Singing Tree's glasses. They looked on all the beams, and they felt between bales of hay, moving some of them when they could. They spent hours searching, but found no glasses. In the evening before it grew dark Mrs. Grant went back and searched again, but again she could not find the glasses.

"Perhaps God has some other plan for us," she said tiredly to her family. "We shall see."

A few days later Mrs. Grant took Singing Tree and Laughing Water to the eye doctor for examinations. When he had finished, the doctor said to Mrs. Grant, "I have good news for you. Your little Indians' eyes are really in fine shape now. Neither of them needs glasses anymore."

"That is good news, doctor," replied Mrs. Grant, "but I don't understand; you told us before that the little one needed glasses. How does it come about that she does not need them now?"

"Just take my word, Mrs. Grant," the doctor said. "The problem with her eyes has been corrected. She doesn't need glasses anymore."

That night Mrs. Grant said to her children, "Just think; if Singing Tree's glasses had not been lost it probably would have been a long time before we found out that she didn't need glasses

105

anymore. I think God kept us from finding the glasses so that we would find this out. Those glasses were quite a worry to me, trying to keep track of them, and there was no sense in her wearing them if she did not need them. God has been good to us in not showing us where they were."

At bedtime Laughing Water said, "Jesus helped you to find the boots, but He didn't help you to find the glasses. Why does He help sometimes and not at other times, Mamma?"

Mrs. Grant smiled warmly. "Our kind Father in heaven sees what is best for us, just as mothers and fathers know what is best for their children," she said. "Sometimes the kind Father says No, and we wonder why; but in a little while we find out and are very thankful to Him for saying No."

Chapter 14

Disappointing Adventures

The Grant home was all hustle and bustle on that early fall morning. Mrs. Grant tried to haul two little brown girls out of bed much earlier than they wanted to wake up. Singing Tree's mop of black hair tumbled all over her face as she sat up and rubbed her eyes, yawned, and stretched. As for Laughing Water, she was very upset.

"Why do I have to get up?" she grumbled. "I don't think the chickens are even awake yet, and they are always the first awake!"

"Oh, they've been up for hours!" Mrs. Grant said, trying to sound cheerful.

"Guess what!" Jamey said through the open doorway. "Something like school is going to happen today!"

The two little Indians stared in wild and wide-eyed wonder. So the day had come at last!

"Hop along to the bathroom and get all that sleepiness out of your eyes with some cold water," Mrs. Grant directed. "Isn't this that wonderful day that you have been wanting to come for a long time?"

About an hour later the hustle, bustle, and grumbling had quieted and everyone was ready to begin the new adventure. The Indians left the house with hugs and kisses for their mother; but, to Mrs. Grant's great astonishment, they had gone just a short way down the drive when she spotted Singing Tree headed for home.

"Whatever is the matter?" she asked. "Did you forget something?"

107

"No," said Singing Tree, sniffling, "I don't want to go to school, after all. It will be hard work, and I'll get my pretty new red dress all dirty when I play on the swings and slides with the kids. I want to stay at home with you, Mamma!"

"Oh, it will be lovely at school!" Mrs. Grant said. "There will be lots of little children for you to play and work with. You'll do coloring, and your teacher will read stories. Once you get there you'll really enjoy it. Look! I see the bus coming along the road on the other side of the river. If you don't hurry to catch up with Laughing Water, you'll miss all the fun of riding with the other children on Mr. Sam's big, rattly bus."

Singing Tree clung to her mother, giving her another big, moist kiss; then she raced off to overtake her sister.

Mrs. Grant walked slowly and thoughtfully into the living room. The house seemed unbelievably quiet. She turned on the phonograph, which began playing beautiful organ music. She leaned back in her favorite chair and smiled a happy kind of smile and told herself, "For a few hours today, I will not need my walking shoes."

That first school day passed more quickly than any day Mrs. Grant could remember. It seemed so short, in fact, that when the kitchen clock said 3:40, she called on the telephone to make sure the clock was telling the truth. She wanted to argue with the recorded voice when it claimed the time was 3:40; but what was the use? The voice refused to answer back.

There was no doubt about the time a few minutes later as she watched out the window while two little Indians walked slowly up the drive in the uncomfortable September heat. Mrs. Grant put on her walking shoes and hurried to meet them.

"Well, what kind of day did both of you have?" she asked, wondering at their lack of excitement as she took one of their hands in each of hers. Laughing Water had nothing to say. Singing Tree looked miserable; her tears began to dribble and then flow.

"Oh, you're not going to cry!" exclaimed Mrs. Grant. "Didn't you like school? Weren't your recesses lots of fun?"

The girls had absolutely no news to report to Mrs. Grant; just

108

stony silence on one side and louder and louder sobs and sniffs on the other. As they toiled up the hill, Mrs. Grant noticed that the pretty red plaid dress which Singing Tree had worried about that morning was now looking as though a cat had chewed on it and a dog with muddy paws had trampled it.

After a cool wash and a change into sun dresses the girls relaxed a little.

"What was the matter with school, Singing Tree?" asked Mrs. Grant as she poured three glasses of cold fruit juice.

"There was a little skinny first-grade kid," said Singing Tree. "He had a mean face, Mamma, and he yelled at me, 'Hello, Nigger! Dirty Nigger! Go back where you came from!'"

Mrs. Grant put down the potato she had just begun to peel and stared at Singing Tree. She opened her mouth to say something, then closed it. Picking up the potato again, she went on peeling with her back to the girls so that they would not see the tear straying on her cheek. Her voice was quiet when she spoke.

"What did *you* say?" she asked.

"I didn't talk to him," said Singing Tree. "I didn't think of anything shootable to say to a mean kid!"

"The word is *suitable*," said Mrs. Grant, glad to grab an extra moment to gain control of her feelings.

Finally Laughing Water spoke. "That wasn't the worst thing, Mamma," she said hoarsely. "He told all the other kids not to play with Singing Tree. He said that good kids don't play with dirty Niggers. Then they all started yelling, 'Go home, dirty Nigger! Go back to where you came from!'"

Now both the girls were weeping. Mrs. Grant left her potato peeling and took them on her lap, rocking them back and forth. She had never before thought of this problem. It had not occurred to her or any of the family that such a thing could happen to the beautiful little Indians whom they already loved so much and who had become like members of the family.

The hands of the copper skillet clock moved on and on until the many tears were spent; then Mrs. Grant began to hum softly, and then to sing the song she had taught to Liza and Peggy and Bonnie and the two little Indians:

" 'My Father is rich in houses and lands;
He holdeth the wealth of the world in His hands!
Of rubies and diamonds, of silver and gold,
His coffers are full—He has riches untold.
I'm a child of the King, a child of the King!
With Jesus, my Saviour, I'm a child of the King!' "

"Even if we have Indian skins we are still God's little kids, aren't we, Mamma?" Singing Tree said, bouncing off her mother's lap.

"You surely are," said Mrs. Grant, trying to hold her face at an angle where the girls could not see another tear welling in her eye. "I want both of you to remember that, all the time. Always remember what Mamma told you about the kind Father loving all children. Remember, too, how I want you never to feel ashamed of being Indians."

Mr. Grant, Celia, and Jamey were shocked when Mrs. Grant told them about Singing Tree's unhappy day at school.

"I think you should talk to her teacher," said Mr. Grant, looking worried. "We can't let that go on. It will ruin school for Singing Tree."

All that second day as Mrs. Grant went about her housework she whispered little prayers for help for Singing Tree. Though just a tiny child, she was having to face a giant, grown-up problem; how would it be, Mrs. Grant wondered, in Singing Trees shoes? The world must look frightening and very ugly to her.

As Lady began to whine and yap at the sound of children's voices away down the hill, Mrs. Grant slipped on her walking shoes and hurried to meet the girls. She was thankful to see that the little shoulders were not as droopy as yesterday.

"How did things go today?" she asked.

"It was the same," Singing Tree said, but no tears came this time. "The kids were yelling, 'Go home, Nigger!' all the recesses. The mean boy threw a rock at me."

"What did *you* say?" asked Mrs. Grant, trying to keep her voice steady.

"I didn't say anything, Mamma," said Singing Tree flatly. "He wouldn't be listening to me, you know. I demember what

110

you said about if Jesus' love is in our hearts we won't be mean. I want Jesus' love in my heart all the time. I tried not to cry about the mean boy. Do you think we ought to say prayers for him so he won't be mean and teach the other kids to be mean?"

"That's a wonderful idea," Mrs. Grant said, taking the child in her arms and squeezing her in a big hug.

Laughing Water began to laugh. The laugh started as the laugh Mrs. Grant had heard when she first heard laughter from Laughing Water, like bubbling water in a clear stream. But this time, it grew and grew until it became a very loud cackle.

Finally, above the cackle came Mrs. Grant's voice. "Laughing Water! Whatever is so funny?"

"You know what a little boy said about me?" asked Laughing Water between cackles. "He yelled to the other kids, 'Hey! Come over here on the playground and see the Mexican girl!' You see, Mamma, he was a new boy. He didn't know me last year. A lot of kids came running, looking at me. They thought I was a Mexican girl, you see! I suppose some of the children did not know what an Indian child looks like, Mamma. It is funny how they don't know an Indian when it used to be the Indians' country, isn't it?"

"I don't see anything terribly funny about that," said Mrs. Grant. "Strange, and a shame, yes, but not funny at all, as far as I am concerned."

On the third day of school Mrs. Turnbull, the teacher who was on playground duty, walked around the corner of the school building in time to hear the little thin boy yell, "Dirty Nigger! Who wants to play with you!" She whisked him into her classroom and, after that magic moment, no one called "Dirty Nigger, go home!" again. School became a happy place for Singing Tree.

On a Saturday night Mrs. Grant said, "I think I'll go to bed early. For some reason, I just don't feel very well."

"If that's the case," said Mr. Grant, "it's a good idea, your going to bed early. Why don't you have a 'sleep-in' for once? We can take care of ourselves. It isn't as if we had to get off to school early."

"Oh, what luxury!" Mrs. Grant thought. Not having to grab to turn off the alarm was something, she always said, that made her feel like a millionaire.

There was a knock on her bedroom door about 9:30 on Sunday morning. "Who?" she called sleepily.

"It's us, Mamma!" called Singing Tree. "We have a gorious apprise for you!"

"Come in," invited Mrs. Grant. "I think you mean glorious surprise, don't you? Ohhhh! You're giving me my breakfast in bed! Aren't I a queen?"

Laughing Water carried a tray on which a plate of fried eggs sat together with toast, a glass of milk, and a little bowl of canned apricots. The eggs were fried crisply dark brown and verged on black at the edges; the toast was black not only on the edges but all over, except for the places where an attempt had been made to scrape the black away. A little of the scrapings from the toast had gone into the glass of milk. The children watched their mother anxiously as she ate and oh, dear! Mrs. Grant ate every speck of that food!

"We thought you'd say it was terrible, Mamma," said Laughing Water, her face gloomy. "Burnt stuff tastes horrible, doesn't it?"

"We did our bestest for you, Mamma," said Singing Tree. "We wanted you to derpreciate it because it was our bestest. It is the first time we made breakfast."

"I know you did your best," Mrs. Grant said with a beaming smile, "and that is why I enjoyed it, even though it was burnt. Anything, when it is done with loving thoughts, brings happiness, you know. That is how Jesus looks on the loving things we do too; even though they don't always turn out as well as we'd like them to, He sees why we wanted to do those loving acts. That is what matters to Him."

Mr. Grant came in, just then, looking worried.

"Is something wrong?" Mrs. Grant asked.

"The new baby calves I brought home on Wednesday don't seem very well," Mr. Grant answered. "I can't understand it; they all looked like such sturdy little fellows, and they were fine last night when I put them to bed. I think I should call Dr. Berkley. They wouldn't suck the milk from their buckets, and they really look down in the dumps."

Singing Tree's face looked cloudy. "Will they die, Daddy?"

"I hope not," said Mr. Grant, "but when tiny calves like that get sick it is difficult to save them."

Singing Tree and Laughing Water gave each other that certain kind of look which Mrs. Grant had noticed the night she found Singing Tree's glasses had vanished. A fearful little chill tickled her backbone, causing her to open her mouth to say something; then she decided not to, at least not yet.

Dr. Berkley shook his head solemnly. "Those little guys have gorged themselves, Mr. Grant. They're just as full as fat little ticks, almost ready to burst. How much did you feed them this morning?"

"That's strange," Mr. Grant said, scratching his head and wrinkling his nose. "I didn't feed them. I tried to, but they wouldn't suck!"

Dr. Berkley whistled a little tune, then hummed a little tune, then he, also, scratched his head and wrinkled his nose.

He even looked as though he thought Mr. Grant was not telling the truth. Suddenly he turned to look at two little wide-eyed Indians and a light seemed to flash in his dark brown eyes.

"Do you suppose, Mr. Grant, that fairies or Mr. Nobody may have fed your calves this morning?" he asked with a huge wink.

Mr. Grant looked surprised and wondered what Dr. Berkley meant, when he, too, noticed the little Indians. "Oh, no! You don't mean—! Laughing Water, did you feed the calves this morning?"

Two Indians stared at the ground.

"We were helping, Daddy," Singing Tree said in a quaking voice. "Mamma was sick and you were sleeping; so we got up early to do everything the bestest way we could."

"How much food did you give them?" asked Mr. Grant.

"They were very hungry calves," said Laughing Water. "We gave them up to the second ring on the bucket like you and Mamma always do, but they were still hungry and cried and chased us, so we mixed some more for them up to the second ring of the buckets again."

113

Dr. Berkley said, "There you have it, Mr. Grant. Overfeeding with a vengeance! Nothing can make a baby calf ill faster than too much to drink."

"Do you think we'll be able to save them?" asked Mr. Grant.

"They're healthy-looking little critters. They might pull through, but I can't promise you anything," Dr. Berkley replied as he got into his car.

Now Mr. Grant took his turn at delivering lectures. He was surprised at the number of sentences and paragraphs he could think of on the topic of why children should ask the permission of parents before doing something for the first time.

It was soon evident that Mr. Grant had not gotten through to the little girls. Their habit of doing things for the first time without adult permission was not yet over. In the late afternoon when Mrs. Grant was up and preparing dinner for her family, Jamey appeared in the kitchen doorway holding a bicycle tire and tube.

"You could never guess what's happened now!" he said.

Mrs. Grant stared at the objects Jamey held.

"You mean to tell me they tried to put the new tire and tube on Singing Tree's bicycle?"

"Right!" said Jamey. "The tube is pinched in exactly thirteen places; at least, that is my modest estimate." Jamey's disgust came from the fact that he had paid for the new tire and tube for Singing Tree's bicycle.

"Win some, lose some," he sighed. "I suppose today was one of those 'lose some' days, Mother. Those three calves look mighty wobbly right now, I might add. I'm glad you didn't lose your breakfast. You were a real soldier, eating those burnt offerings they presented you this morning."

"Oh, well," Mrs. Grant sighed. "We learn by experience, you know. I remember a little boy years ago who made a few blunders while doing things he thought were helpful."

Jamey grinned sheepishly. "That's funny," he said; "I can't remember anything like that."

As Mrs. Grant was seeing the girls into bed for the night, Laughing Water said, "We tried to help you all day, Mamma, but we didn't do so well, did we?"

114

"Everyone makes mistakes; even grown-up people make them," Mrs. Grant comforted. "There are some things little children cannot do alone, you know, so grown-up people must teach them. Usually, as we grow older, we do better, you understand. If you *do* happen to make a mistake, it is very important that you learn from it and do much better next time."

"Yes, Mamma," said Singing Tree. "It is very inpertent to make mistakes, isn't it? That way, you can eat burnt food and it doesn't burn your mouth, does it?"

"Oh, dear!" sighed Mrs. Grant. "The end of a perfect day!"

"We'll pray for the little baby calves not to die, Mamma," said Laughing Water. "I think the kind Father knew we were trying to help, didn't He?"

"I'm sure He did," said Mrs. Grant. "He knows why we do everything and is glad to see His love working in our hearts."

Chapter 15

Henny Penny Has Troubles

"I had bad dreams last night, Mamma," Singing Tree said as she dragged her chair to the table to eat breakfast. "I dreamed that a big giant squished me all up in his hand and laughed at me and said, 'There, you little Indian! I made you the right size, now!' Every time I would try to run away he would squish me again and laugh. It was a mean laugh, Mamma."

"How would it be just to forget the bad dream?" Mrs. Grant suggested. "Think of something nice instead, like the pretty autumn leaves on the trees that we can see through the kitchen window and the little birds feeding on the grass seeds under the trees; about the nice food you have for breakfast—"

"We're lucky little children, aren't we, Mamma?" said Laughing Water. "We get all the good food we need. I saw a picture in a magazine of poor little children who don't have enough to eat. I pray for all the poor little hungry children, that Jesus will give them food. When I'm a grown-up lady I will be like you, Mamma," she added. "I will take care of poor little children who have no mothers and fathers, and I will give them a nice home and love them. I'll teach them about the kind Father in heaven too."

"That's what I'll do too, Mamma," said Singing Tree. "If every big lady and man would help the poor little kids, soon there wouldn't be any poor little kids, would there?"

Mrs. Grant smiled happily. "That's wonderful," she said. "I would be the happiest mother in the world if I saw my little Indians growing up to help needy little children. You would truly be doing the work of Jesus."

116

"Guess what!" exclaimed Jamey, arriving by way of the kitchen door.

"You found Henny Penny's nest?" asked both Indians at the same instant.

"Now, aren't you good guessers today!" Jamey said. "That's half the 'guess-what'; now guess the other half."

When nobody offered an answer, Jamey answered his own question. "The calves are looking brighter today, and all of them sucked a little of their milk. I think maybe they might pull through all right."

"We asked Jesus to help the little critters get better," said Singing Tree. "Jesus knows when little critters are sick."

"Just where did the child hear *that* word?" Mrs. Grant asked Jamey.

"Dr. Berkley said 'critters,' said Singing Tree. "It means sick calves, Mamma. I'm really surprised that you don't know words like 'critters.' "

"The word 'critters,' " Jamey explained, "does not mean baby calves; it means creatures."

"That's right, Jamey," agreed Singing Tree. "That's it! Critters is critters, so critters is baby calves, even if they are not sick."

"Let's change the subject," said Mrs. Grant. "This conversation seems to be getting nowhere. How many eggs were in Henny Penny's nest, and where did you find it?"

"In the hay," Jamey told his mother. "I've searched for days for that nest, and I must hand it to Henny Penny; she's a shrewd little Bantam if ever there was one. She found a small tunnel through the hay, right at the bottom of the pile of bales. We never would have found those eggs if I had not been there to see her come out of the tunnel. She flew from the barn to the ground and then started to cackle much too loud for such a tiny hen. There were seventeen eggs in the nest."

"Since some animal must have taken the rooster, I think we should lock her in with the Leghorns," Mrs. Grant said. "There seems to be no other suitable place to give her protection. It would be fun to be able to find her eggs every day so that the girls could have tiny eggs for breakfast."

SINGING TREE AND LAUGHING WATER

Henny Penny scared the bigger hens when she was put in their pen. They darted here and there, screeching and cackling and shedding feathers. Not that the little Bantam did anything to scare the hens; they just feared her because she was different. They made it clear that they did not like the little brown-and-black speckled hen. After a few hours, when their fright had worn off, the hens attacked Henny Penny, pecking her comb and flapping their wings over her.

"You are not welcome!" they seemed to cackle.

After three days Henny Penny was no more welcome than she had been at the beginning. Singing Tree and Laughing Water came running to the house after school crying, "Mamma! Come do something! The Leghorns are pulling out Henny Penny's tail! They're being mean and cruel to her. Come quickly!"

By the time Mrs. Grant reached the chicken house, poor little Henny Penny was crouched on the ground with not one beautiful tail feather left. For several days Henny Penny scarcely ate any food, and when she did eat she waited until all the big white hens had gobbled up as much of the food as they wanted. After they had pulled out all her tail feathers, the Leghorns paid no more attention to Henny Penny's living with them; they neither hurt her nor befriended her. But they made it plain that Henny Penny did not belong.

"Poor little Henny Penny," Singing Tree said. "I know how she feels. It is like the kids did to me when the mean little boy called me 'Nigger' and told the others not to play with me. Poor little Henny Penny is sad. Do you think we can teach the big hens to be kind to her?"

"That is doubtful," said Mrs. Grant. "With people, it is different. People have understanding; so if they really want to they can learn to love all other kinds of people, no matter how different they might be from them."

Singing Tree raced down the aisle of a large supermarket. "Mamma, Mamma," she panted, almost completely out of breath. "Guess what! There is a lady back there getting some canned corn, and she told Laughing Water and me we are beautiful.

*The Leghorns were pulling out
  Henny Penny's tail.*

Just beautiful big dolls, the lady said, Mamma. A lot of ladies say we are beautiful when they see us in stores. Laughing Water and me is beautiful, aren't we, Mamma?"

"Steady, now," said Mrs. Grant, ignoring Singing Tree's poor grammar. "Just *why* do you think you are so beautiful?"

"Well, we must be, Mamma," said Singing Tree, sounding a little let down. "How else would a lot of people say Laughing Water and me is beautiful if we wasn't beautiful?"

"It's a long, long story," Mrs. Grant said as she often did when she did not have the time to spend in explaining some problem to the girls. "Perhaps tonight at bedtime we'll talk about this again."

"All right," she said when bedtime came. "Mamma has been trying very hard to teach you that it isn't what people look like on the outside that matters very much, but rather what is in their thoughts and hearts that really matters. Right?"

"Yes, Mamma," agreed the girls.

"All right," she said again. "Thinking of that we must remember that it really doesn't matter if people call you 'dirty Nigger' or 'beautiful,' does it? Some people like your appearance and some don't; to some you are one thing and to some you are another. What is felt about how you look, then, is a changing thing and means very little. The very, very important thing is what is to be found inside of you. I have told you that many times. We are beautiful only as kindness and the love of Jesus flow from our hearts and minds to others. Will you *please* remember?"

"You've said it too many times, Mamma," Singing Tree said sleepily. "How else couldn't we derember?"

"That is quite a complicated question," Mrs. Grant said, and she, too, sounded sleepy. "I'm afraid I'll let it go as possibly unintelligible."

"Oh, Mamma," said Singing Tree, springing up in her bed as wide-awake as a child could be. "That is a splendisheous word, and I want to say it every day. 'Posservlyununtergable.' The little mean boy at school will be surprised when I say that to the teacher."

Mrs. Grant laughed as she bent to kiss Singing Tree good night. "I have a feeling your teacher will be surprised also," she said and then turned to kiss Laughing Water.

Laughing Water said, "We haven't said prayers yet, Mamma."

"I think I shall say an Indian prayer for you tonight," said Mrs. Grant. "It is a Navajo prayer. The Navajos were a family of desert Indians, just as the Zuñis were desert Indians. There are still Navajos living south of us in the desert. You close your eyes and listen carefully to the words of the prayer. Sometime when we aren't so sleepy Mamma will teach the prayer to you.

'In beauty may I walk;
With beauty before me, may I walk;
With beauty behind me, may I walk;
With beauty above me, may I walk;
With beauty all around me, may I walk;
In beauty may my walk be finished;
In beauty may my walk be finished.'

"That lovely prayer will be answered as long as the love of Jesus lives in us," Mrs. Grant said, switching off the girls' light. "Having His love with you makes the whole world beautiful."

Chapter 16

"I Think the Kind Father Brought Us Here!"

Another evening at bedtime, after Mrs. Grant had read the children their Bible story, Laughing Water said, "Mamma, there is something I don't understand. You told us that Jesus came to this world to teach people how to love each other; well, the other day at church the teacher told us Jesus came to die for us. Why did you tell us one thing and the teacher tell us something different? I don't understand what the lady meant when she said Jesus came to die for us."

"It might seem that we said two different things," Mrs. Grant answered, "but when I tell you a story I think you will understand that we were really meaning the same thing."

"Ah! Goody!" said Singing Tree. "Two stories in one night!"

"Well, I want you to listen very carefully so you will remember this story as long as you live," Mrs. Grant said.

"Once there were two girls—"

"What were their names, Mamma? Laughing Water and Singing Tree?"

"No, as a matter of fact, their names were Sarah and Jane," Mrs. Grant answered. "Sarah was a big girl, bigger than you. She was twelve years old, and her little sister, Jane, was six years old. Their mother, Mrs. Needham, owned a beautiful old china doll named Lottie. Lottie had belonged to Mrs. Needham's grandmother when she was a little girl and to Mrs. Needham's mother when she was a little girl, so, you see, the china doll was very, very old and very, very precious to Mrs. Needham. Because it was made of china like Mamma's best dinner dishes, the doll could be easily broken if it were dropped or bumped on anything hard. Mrs. Needham did not want her china doll to be broken. At special times

122

like birthdays or Thanksgiving or Christmas she would take Lottie from the cupboard in her room and allow the girls to sit on their beds to play with Lottie for a little time. Of course, Sarah and Jane took every care with Lottie.

"One evening when Jane was snuggled in bed for the night, Mrs. Needham went next door to visit her sick neighbor. Sarah was working on her homework, and Mr. Needham was reading a book; the house seemed very quiet. As Jane lay in her little pink bed with its frilled pink spread, she thought about Lottie. She longed to hold the precious doll in her arms and look at the pretty blue painted eyes. The longing grew until she decided that she would get Lottie down from the cupboard herself. She tiptoed into her mother's room; and, standing on a chair, she opened the cupboard door to find Lottie wrapped very carefully in fine tissue paper. Quickly she took the doll from the cupboard and scurried back to her room. She took the soft tissue paper off Lottie and put it under her pillow so that it would be where she could find it when she wanted to rewrap Lottie.

"What joy it was to hold Lottie in her lovely lavender satin dress with rows and rows of tiny frills trimmed with cream-colored lace! Jane held Lottie for a long time, but it did not seem a long time at all to Jane, she was having such a lovely time. She was surprised and frightened when she heard her mother say, 'I saw Jane's light was still on as I came from Mrs. Fletcher's house. I feel sure I switched it off when I said good night to her. I must go upstairs and see what she is doing.'

"Oh, dear! Jane felt very frightened now. Mother would be really displeased because she had disobeyed by taking Lottie from her safe hiding place.

" 'I know,' thought Jane, 'I will hide Lottie under my blankets, and I will pretend to be asleep when Mother comes. She will switch off the light and never know that Lottie is in bed with me. When Mother goes back downstairs I will creep back to her bedroom and put Lottie back in the cupboard.'

"Jane's plan worked very well. Mrs. Needham looked in on her and then switched off the light; but, instead of going back downstairs, she went to her bedroom.

123

"Jane didn't understand how it happened, but the next thing she knew the sun was shining brightly through her open window and breakfast dishes were making little clinking sounds downstairs. Forgetting all about Lottie's being in bed with her, she threw back the covers to jump out of bed, and crash! Lottie was on the floor in at least twenty pieces. Mrs. Needham and Sarah came running up the stairs to see what had happened.

" 'Whatever was—' Mrs. Needham did not finish the question. 'Oh, Lottie! My precious Lottie!' she cried. 'How did she get broken? And why was she out of the cupboard?'

" 'I got her when you were away last night, Mother,' said Jane. 'I wanted to put her back in the cupboard again, but I went to sleep and forgot she was in the bed with me. When I threw back the covers, she fell on the floor and broke.'

"Mrs. Needham's face looked very pained and sad. 'You were a disobedient girl, Jane,' she said. 'I am sad, really sad, about Lottie, but I am sadder because you did such a wrong thing in disobeying Mother. I must punish you because you disobeyed.'

"Jane began to cry. She knew that she had done wrong, and she felt sad and sorry about having been disobedient. She also felt sorry about Lottie's being broken. Worst of all, she could not stand the thought of a whipping from her mother.

"Sarah stood, teary-eyed, watching her little sister's misery. She felt very sorry for her. 'I wish Mother wouldn't whip Jane,' she thought. 'Oh, what can I do so that Jane will not be whipped? What can I do? Oh, I know,' Sarah thought. 'I will ask Mother to whip me instead of Jane. I will take Jane's whipping!'

" 'Mother, I will take Jane's whipping,' said Sarah. 'Please, Mother. I know she deserves the whipping, but I can't stand to see her whipped. Please, Mother, whip me instead!'

" 'Is that what you really want?' Mrs. Needham asked, very surprised.

" 'Oh, yes, Mother. I love little Jane, and I don't want to see her punished like that.'

" 'All right, Sarah,' Mrs. Needham said. 'You are a wonderful sister to little Jane.'

"Jane cried and cried when she saw Sarah being whipped.

She wished that she had not let Sarah take her punishment. "Mrs. Needham sat down with the girls after the whipping, her arms about both of them, and she said to Jane, 'I hope you will always remember how Sarah loved you enough to suffer your whipping in your place, because that is how our dear Saviour, Jesus, died for you and for all of us.

" 'Everyone has sinned and been disobedient to the kind Father, but Jesus said, "Dear Father, I love them all, very much. I know that you have said that those who have done wrong must have their punishment by dying forever, but I will die in their place so that they will not die forever."

" 'So Jesus died on the cross so that, even though we might die for a little while, He will raise us up when He comes back to this earth again, just as He was raised up after death, and He will let us live forever.'

"Jane loved her big sister more than she had ever loved her because of the love she showed in taking the whipping for her," Mrs. Grant said.

Singing Tree and Laughing Water lay very, very quiet in their beds.

Mrs. Grant said, "The lady at the church was right when she said Jesus came to die for us, and Mamma was right, too, because, in dying for us, Jesus showed how much He really loves us and how much we must love each other; even dying for each other, if that be necessary sometimes."

"Did Jesus take the whipping for all the little kids and people in the world?" asked Singing Tree in a very quiet voice.

"Yes, He did," answered Mrs. Grant, "and the Bible tells us that whoever wants to may come to Him for the gift of everlasting life which He bought for them when He died. He has promised us a lovely home with His Father in heaven if we love Him and want to live with Him. Everything will be beautiful and happy there. Some of the old-fashioned Indians used to talk about a happy hunting ground; that was their idea about what heaven would be like."

"I love Jesus for dying for me," Laughing Water said with tears popping into her eyes.

125

"I do, too, Mamma," Singing Tree said in a quiet little voice. Mrs. Grant said, "We must keep in our hearts always our love for Jesus; then we will always be loving and kind to everyone."

"Even to mean little kids that say 'dirty Nigger'?"

"That's right," said Mrs. Grant. "And, you know something? It would be a good idea for us to forget all about that. It isn't worth remembering. Let us forgive the little boy, just as our kind Father forgives us and still loves us when we do unkind and mean things. Don't you remember that we agreed once that we should pray for the little boy?"

"That's right, Mamma," agreed Singing Tree. "We said that was the bestest thing to do with the problem."

Late on a winter night Mrs. Grant awoke suddenly. Had the telephone rung? She listened, but she heard no ringing telephone. Had someone rung the door chimes? She listened, but no chimes sounded. Because Mrs. Grant felt uneasy in those waking moments she slipped silently out of bed and opened and closed the bedroom door quietly so that Mr. Grant would not be disturbed.

Coals still glowed in the big white living-room fireplace, so Mrs. Grant drew up a comfortable chair and watched the bright orange coals, imagining pictures in the flickering shadows of the coals. A strong wind moaned in the chimney and sighed through the branches of the elm trees in the front yard. Mrs. Grant had been watching the fire for a long time, when she began to hear soft little pattering sounds like something hitting lightly against the glass of the big picture windows. She drew back the heavy window drapes to see big snowflakes swirling and dashing themselves against the glass. When she switched on the outdoor lights, she could see that the elms, once bare of branch, now wore a dainty covering of soft snow. A blanket of snow covered the ground too, and the snow twinkled in the soft light.

"Oh, thank You, loving Father, for the beautiful world," she whispered, "but remember those poor little ones who are cold and hungry and for whom the winter world is frightening and not beautiful."

Mrs. Grant stopped her prayer suddenly. The thought came

126

to her that at that moment in one of the bedrooms upstairs lay two little children who could possibly be cold and hungry and unloved that very hour if she and Mr. Grant and their family had not opened their home to them. She continued talking to her kind Father whom she knew and loved so well. "Thank You, dear Father, for sending them to us," she went on. "You know this really wasn't our plan, but we see the things we should do when You lead us. And now they have brought us such joy, and we love them so much."

"Oh!" she said to herself. "I forgot to lock the kitchen door before I went to bed; maybe that was the reason I awoke with a start. My mind seemed to know there was something I should have done, but had not done."

The bolt on the door clicked ever so quietly; just a baby click, but Singing Tree heard it.

"Mamma!" she cried. "Is it you?"

"Yes," Mrs. Grant answered in a soft voice, hoping not to disturb Laughing Water; but when Mrs. Grant stepped into the bedroom, she, too, sprang up in bed, blinking like an old owl.

"You go to sleep again," Mrs. Grant told the girls. "I just remembered I hadn't kept my promise to Singing Tree to lock the kitchen door every night, so I came to lock it."

"That's right, Mamma," said Singing Tree. "I don't want to be afraid that someone will come and steal our nice sweet Mamma in the night."

Mrs. Grant switched off the light as she said, "Back to sleep, now, both of you."

"Mamma, come back!" cried Singing Tree. "It is very important. Did I say it right that time, Mamma?"

"At *last!*" said Mrs. Grant. "Three cheers! I can't wait to tell Jamey!"

"Come and sit on my bed, Mamma," said Singing Tree, now very wide-awake while Laughing Water still blinked uncertainly. "What I have to say is important and you must listen." Mrs. Grant sat on Singing Tree's bed.

"Mamma, you are our real, *real* mother, aren't you?" said Singing Tree happily.

127

"Well, no. How can I be your mother when I am not an Indian?" she asked in surprise.

"You don't underspand!" complained Singing Tree.

"It's *understand*," growled Laughing Water.

"What is it I don't understand?" asked Mrs. Grant.

"This is how it is," replied Singing Tree. "Our real mother is the one that borned us, but you are our real, *real* mother because you love us. It's the ones that love kids that are the real, *real* mothers, don't you see?"

Singing Tree threw back her covers and dived into Mrs. Grant's lap, smothering her face and neck with big wet kisses.

"I love my real, *real* mother!" she said.

Laughing Water bounded out of bed and gave Mrs. Grant the same kind of treatment.

"Sometimes I think, Mamma," said Laughing Water, still shy at times, and shy now. "I think a lot about why we came to live with you and Daddy and Celia and Jamey and Richard. I think the kind Father brought us here because He knew you would love us and you'd teach us about Him. I'm glad we came here to live."

Mrs. Grant gave each of the girls a last squeeze and kissed them lightly on their foreheads, then tucked them into bed for the second time that night.

"Sleep well," she said, afraid to tell them of the beautiful snow that lay beneath their windows because she knew they would never go back to sleep that night if they knew.

As Mrs. Grant tiptoed to her bedroom, she passed the cupboard in which she kept her walking shoes. Creeping back to it, she opened the door which squeaked just a little. There were her walking shoes, worn down at the heels and scuffed on the toes. She stood several minutes gazing at them, and then she smiled a wide smile.

"Mrs. Grant, perhaps you won't need your walking shoes much longer," she told herself.

128